Uncut Funk

In an awesome meeting of minds, cultural theorists Stuart Hall and
bell hooks met for a series of wide-ranging conversations on what Hall
sums up as "life, love, death, sex." From the trivial to the profound,
across boundaries of age, sexualities and genders, hooks and Hall dis-
sect topics and themes of continual contemporary relevance, including
feminism, home and homecoming, class, black masculinity, family, politics, relationships and teaching. In their fluid and honest dialogue they
push and pull each other as well as the reader, and the result is a book
that speaks to the power of conversation as a place of critical pedagogy.

A cultural critic, an intellectual, and a feminist writer, **bell hooks** is best
known for classic books including *Feminist Theory*, *Bone Black*, *All About
Love*, *Rock My Soul*, *Belonging*, *We Real Cool*, *Where We Stand*, *Teaching to
Transgress*, *Teaching Community*, *Outlaw Culture* and *Reel to Real*. hooks is
Distinguished Professor in Residence in Appalachian Studies at Berea
College, and resides in her home state of Kentucky.

Stuart Hall (1932–2014) was born in Kingston, Jamaica and came to
England in 1951. He was a pioneering cultural theorist, political activist,
and founding editor of the *New Left Review*. He was one of the most
influential and adventurous critical thinkers of the last half century,
widely recognised as a key figure in the development of cultural studies.

First published 2018
by Routledge
711 Third Avenue, New York, NY 10017

and by Routledge
2 Park Square, Milton Park, Abingdon, Oxon OX14 4RN

Routledge is an imprint of the Taylor & Francis Group, an informa business

Library of Congress Cataloging-in-Publication Data
Names: hooks, bell, 1952– author. | Hall, Stuart, 1932–2014, author.
Title: Uncut funk : a contemplative dialogue / bell hooks and Stuart Hall ;
    foreword by Paul Gilroy.
Description: New York : Routledge, 2018.
Identifiers: LCCN 2017021207 | ISBN 9781138102064 (hardback) |
    ISBN 9781138102101 (pbk.) | ISBN 9781315103624 (eBook)
Subjects: LCSH: Blacks—Politics and government. | African
    Americans—Politics and government. | Political culture.
Classification: LCC DT16.5 .H66 2018 | DDC 306.2089/96—dc23
LC record available at https://lccn.loc.gov/2017021207

ISBN: 978-1-138-10206-4 (hbk)
ISBN: 978-1-138-10210-1 (pbk)
ISBN: 978-1-315-10362-4 (ebk)

Typeset in Garamond
by Apex CoVantage, LLC

Printed and bound by CPI Group (UK) Ltd, Croydon, CR0 4YY

"I want my funk uncut."

—*George Clinton*

Contents

Foreword

Reading this conversation makes it impossible to overlook how the language of black political culture has lately been impoverished. The insurgent poetry of social transformation has been flattened and the agenda of liberation curtailed. Today, they are being squeezed so that they can fit the minimal space provided by soundbites and hashtags, tweets and memes, likes and follows. An essentially docile, computer-mediated solidarity may be becoming the norm. Digital networks arise from the transmission of spectacular horrors and the mainstreamed choreography of black resistance, but they often create nothing more than the mirage of a movement. On screen, racism, capitalism and militarism appear intractable. Off screen, large-scale mobilizations occur swiftly and then quickly evaporate. The racial order stagnates or seems to be worsening. Giving voice to alternative and oppositional ways of living and thinking becomes progressively more difficult. Fatigue and anxiety set in. The radical tradition gets routinely invoked, but it is depthless. History becomes a mere backstory, sparsely populated by sparkling, celebrity icons. This accelerating world has made it hard to even imagine that bell hooks and Stuart Hall were ever in real-time conversation, talking and listening to each other in the same room.

Of course, their dialogue was the product of a particular conjuncture. The words and concepts they employ were addressed to the historical processes that formed them, but the ideas are still reverberating.

As they travel towards us down the decades, they have acquired additional resonance. By referring us to its remote sources, their exchange can help to recover and sharpen the historical sensibility of today's readers. These discussions of intellectual life, masculinity and femininity, patriarchy and psychoanalysis take us to the boundary of our own sense of political and generational time. The voices of hooks and Hall sound contemporary. Their carefully spoken responses and vivid hopes are not only a valuable contribution to the dusty archive of an ebbing movement, but might still be important for its future course.

The enduring worth of this exercise is connected to its dialogic form. Conversation not only captures the unusual openness and generosity of both participants but also enacts a rare and precious possibility, namely that together black women and men can create and inhabit an ideal space of free and equal communication. We are well acquainted with that possibility from other vernacular settings where collective or collaborative work and play not only create pleasure, but also embolden those who act in concert and respond to suffering with solidarity. Here, we discover that dissident intellectuals can also be joyful, loving and critical even when they are reflecting on the most difficult, intimate questions of family life, home and kinship. Set aside today's anxiousness and paranoia about whether the correct concepts and phrases are being used, and we may be able to learn from the context of trust that was transacted. In other words, this discussion provides a practical pedagogic example to a radical culture that is now less able to manage the internal disagreements that inevitably arise along generational, gendered and tactical lines.

The evident discipline and formality of the conversational format command the close attention of readers who are invited to appreciate the tone and timbre of these interlocked voices in the same spirit with which the participants listened carefully to each other. Counterpoint their existential duet with the classic, soulful declamations of Donny and Roberta, Aretha and Benson or Bobby Womack and Patti Labelle and you will begin to see the effort concealed behind a sheen of apparent ease. The mutual attentiveness required by the improvised movement of paired voices is educative. It encourages us to practice a deep listening and perhaps to indulge in a slower, more contemplative kind of reading than the illuminated screen will permit.

Contemporary readers may have to do a little bit of translation. The US-centric liturgy of generic, internet-friendly identity-talk is entirely absent. It was not a factor when these dialogues took place. There are no casual invocations here of either privilege or victimage. The common-sense that projects intersectionality into political ontology is challenged implicitly. It is answered with an alternative rendering of intersectional analysis as a vital, dynamic *method* capable of illuminating the struggle critically to interpret a forbiddingly complex world so that it might be altered for the better. That optimistic approach means grasping how, in Hall's terms, different contradictions and conflicts become articulated together in specific, historical and economic circumstances.

As globalization intensified, African American culture was acquiring new kinds of value far from the conditions and the people that produced it. Its custodians and brokers, mostly drawn from the generation that had desegregated elite U.S. educational institutions, were finding a new voice and encountering an unprecedented degree of media attention. A few, supposedly exceptional black intellectuals were coming under a spotlight that ancestors like Du Bois and Anna Julia Cooper did not have to contend with. Their impossible predicament was increasingly being acknowledged, often as an exotic, if morbidly prestigious, item on the trophy shelves of corporate multiculturalism.

Our two conversationalists meet in the rubble of past defeats. The residue of earlier countercultures provides a backdrop for their exchanges. Some of the theoretical debates that were alive at that point have now faded or lost their purchase on the world, but Frantz Fanon's writing supplies an enduring presence—a conceptual compass effective in their time and in ours. His interventions provide a cornerstone for this dialogue, which is oriented politically by events like the Nation of Islam's Million Man March.

Most importantly, when this conversation took place, the personal could still be political without becoming hostage to disabling narcissism. Readers are encouraged to be acquainted with the rebalancing of black Atlantic protest and affirmation during the 1990s. After Black Power, it would be distinguished by the public pursuit of a new, firmly feminist settlement between women and men. Sternly conscious of class relations, sexualities and gender, these speakers were bonded by their shared commitment to explore what that emergent arrangement would involve. These are intellectuals connected by their opposition to inertia-inducing anti-intellectualism, but their conversation is built, above all, upon common determination to find ways of acting politically that are in tune not only with feminist standpoints, but also with a dogged feminist insistence upon the transformation of everyday life.

That task could not be undertaken without a complex understanding of black subjects as ontologically deep, complex in their desires and desperately in need of the comforts provided, on one side, by the process of writing, and on the other, by varieties of psychotherapeutic support: spiritual as well as secular. In a further acknowledgment of the unruly psychic forces in play, these discussions endeavor to make something useful out of the complex class transitions and transformative, migratory journeys made by both speakers. Those autobiographies of displacement are used to bridge generational and experiential divisions. Hall and hooks are entirely unafraid to scrutinize areas of private life that can still be difficult to acknowledge, in particular, the significance of health and sickness, chronic infirmity and death. Their concluding address to mortality provides a final, fundamental theme. It is a key to the leveling, radical morality of this project. Throughout, they refuse to be pushed out of this fleeting, mortal world into the brightly lit realm of the special and the exalted. Self-consciously, their dialogue helps to dismantle the podium on which they have been placed by contingency rather than their undoubted, individual talents. That unusual modesty enhances the power of this conversation. Today, it is welcome encouragement to salvage some worthwhile political habits that have been lost during the intervening decades.

Paul Gilroy

Preface

Meeting black British intellectuals, artists and/or critical thinkers was a defining moment in my life. Hanging out, talking, sharing stories, engaging in sweet dialectical exchange ushered me into a community of committed, engaged thinkers that had heretofore been absent from my life. Stuart Hall was a central figure for all of us. Unlike many brilliant academicians, he was gracious, open and willing to be patient with intellectual newcomers. Deeply committed to the realization of a union between theory and practice, he lived his politics. Awed by the scope of his intellectual insights, I was humbled by his willingness to talk with me. We met often in London. It was a hot summer in 1996. We met for traditional afternoon English tea at a grand hotel and we talked.

I have always been fascinated by the meeting of minds that takes place between two individuals who among the diversity of conversations might never truly speak to one another. Stuart Hall and I had many conversations. Despite our abundance of words, there is a tenderness, a sweetness to our conversation, a moment of private and public revelation that adds new dimensions to our talking to one another and our work. Given that he died much too soon, I shall be ever grateful that we had this time together.

bell hooks

Dialogue between bell hooks and Stuart Hall

bell: For me, conversation is a place of learning. I love a good conversation. It's something I live for, one of the real pleasures of life, and yet, I find as I grow older it is more difficult to have a good conversation.

Stuart: Conversation matters to me a lot, too, although, I don't always say I live for conversation. I live for narrative. Of course, conversation is a lot about narrative, but there are many other kinds of conversations. I find that the conversations that I quite like are those where people are telling me stories about themselves, where there is an element of the confessional. I like to have narrative rehearsed. I like everyday conversation. For instance, my son comes in, and he is terribly tired. He has just been making a film about Brixton. He was there with Mandela. I haven't seen him in a week, and I say, "How's it going?" He says, "Ahh, I'm definitely tired. I don't know if I can bring myself to talk about this." How do you read this when you're hungry for narrative? When I go home in the evening, I want Catherine to tell me about her day, who phoned, and what were the small things that have made up her day. I am not only interested in the big things of life. Perhaps this is different than conversation.

bell: I believe that is conversation. Conversation has a polyphonic variety. You can move in it from the mundane to the profound. It ranges from lessons to be learned about the mundane to something that is deeper and more exciting. I have been thinking about growing up in a world of folks who never learned how to read or write, or folks who didn't read much, an intense world of non-readers and non-writers. What I remember most about that world is this passion of conversation. Just as you are pointing out, there were always extensive narratives about the weather. My grandparents would rise at the crack of dawn, they would turn on the radio, then carry on these conversations which involved talking back to the radio, talking to each other, and talking about the upcoming day.

Stuart: Now as you say that, I am reminded of a childhood memory which I hadn't thought about before. I lived with my family in Kingston. For a lot of reasons, we were the advanced, modern folks who had gone to the big city. My father worked in an electric company, and my mother was intent on status and going up in the world. I found this, for various reasons, a very forbidding place in which to grow up. The place I loved going to was my father's place in the country, in Old Harbour, which is outside of Kingston. It's not very beautiful. It's on the south side of Jamaica which is the flat, dry side, not the romantic northern coast. It is not a tourist area. It is just a little, dusty, country town. They had this very pretty, not quite gingerbread, but almost gingerbread, very small home. It was my grandmother's home (my father's mother), who I am very much like. The house was full of aunts, because my father and his brother got married and moved away. Of the five aunts only one got married and left. This was a house of unmarried but strong and varied women. They were all different from one another. My aunt, who was a teacher, died last year at 105. She was teaching on her back verandah at age 102. My favorite aunt was Post Mistress.

I loved to go to Old Harbour at Christmas. I remember that I didn't enjoy Christmas day which we celebrated in Kingston. It was for fashionable folks. But then on Boxing Day we would go to Old Harbour. It was a country Christmas, but I just thought it was wonderful. The best moment was after Christmas dinner when, as a child, I would go and lay down on this big bed and listen to the aunts talking with my mother about the village gossip. I thought it was just wonderful. Even though I didn't know the people they spoke of I really thought this was just wonderful. It was like a continually unrolling serial. Until now, I hadn't thought about how those moments mark a space where I learned to love people telling me about their everyday life in conversation. It makes sense because that place was a very powerful repository of positive things. It is a positive pole in my childhood. All the negative things circle around my own family's home while the positive circles around my aunts' and my grandmother's home.

bell: You just made me think of how we always say it is a dangerous thing in our house to say anything. For instance, in our little, tiny house, after we eat everyone lays out on different beds to rest, but they are also listening. So from any different corner or room you might get feedback when you thought that you were just talking to one other person. Everyone feels that if you have something that you really want to keep private—

Stuart: You're best not to say it!

bell: Yes, and as a country girl I went away to college thinking that college was going to be this place for these kinds of conversations. It was as if I thought that college was going to replace the discussions of our little town and our neighborhoods with ideas, but that we were still going to be rising early in the morning to sit and to chat. I remember the lack of spaces of conversation as one of my deepest disappointments when I arrived at Stanford. Evidently, at one time, they had designated rooms where people could get together to have tea and talk.

Stuart: Yes, and when you arrived they were no longer used in that way. I don't know that I knew enough about college even to imagine it.

bell: It was because I didn't know what it was like that I was imagining it.

Stuart: Yes. I must say, not all the time, but many of the years I spent at Oxford, and I was there a long time, six years, were times of extreme and intense intellectual and political conversation. It was where the New Left started, and all of those people were around. We had a big student house where people lived, and it was always full of a cross section of people of the Caribbean, people from the Left, people studying literature, people in art school, not just people from the university. It was a place of very, very intense variety, and intense conversation. If I had gone with the expectation for conversation, it was in a way met.

bell: Do you think this had to do with the times?

Stuart: Yes, this was the late fifties and the sixties. I don't want to be too romantic about it either, because there were other things that I absolutely hated about it. I didn't want to go to Oxford, and I hated it by the time I left, so I don't want to paint it in a rosy glow. However, this place was where *Universities and Left Review* was first started, and it was where I made an independent life for the first time. I left home and went to college where they looked after you for a year. Then I moved out into a student house where we made an alternative center—a radical, political, literary center—and battled against official Oxford and all it stood for. All of this gave it an intellectual intensity. It was really very exciting.

bell: As someone who came from a working, poor environment to Stanford, I always had to work while attending school to earn money for books and living expenses. This put me in a space of "would be" young intellectual in the everyday work setting, and one of the ways that I dealt with that setting was to have conversations. I could be sitting as a telephone operator at my microphone all day, and in the meantime galvanizing everybody into a certain kind of conversation about our lives. When I started writing *Ain't I a Woman?* I was working at the telephone company and talking with all of these women who worked there about their perceptions of black womanhood. That was a real important space. It's because of these experiences that I felt conversation is a place of potential pedagogy. When people are seated together at lunch time, whether you're from a different class or not, there is a possibility of sharing in conversation.

Stuart: Yes, sharing across those boundaries. One of the nice things about conversation, as opposed to conferences and fixed formalized occasions, is, of course, its fluidity. It can move from the trivial to the profound, in and out, across boundaries of sexualities and genders, boundaries of experience. It gives you a sense of the dialogic, of conversation as exchange.

bell: The other day a black, Southern, male plumber came to my house, and I was saying to him, "I can't keep my tub clean!" He said, "Do you have some cleanser?", and I said, "Oh, I've tried cleanser." Then I brought him the cleanser that he demanded. He cleaned a little circle, and then said, "Ah, this is a trick. This is just about getting me to clean your tub." We then began a conversation about gender and roles.

Stuart: Which you couldn't have done any other way. If you had proposed it as a formal topic of exchange it wouldn't have got off the ground.

bell: I was going to lunch with Anthony Appiah that day so I was saying to him that I had to get out of there and go to lunch. He asked me, "Who are you going to lunch with, the man in your life?" I said, "Actually I'm going to lunch with a gay, male friend." He then told me to scratch that, and that he was married, but that he could be "my special friend." That started another whole conversation about living in the Village, and what gayness means in terms of friendship. This has been something that has continually intrigued me as a thinker, the possibility of engaging knowledge across different kinds of boundaries. I have been somewhat saddened by the fact that my life became more centered around institutions—the university has become harder for me to have certain kinds of conversations. I have been thinking about the way the act of praying for talk on the formal lecture circuit is so negating of conversation. Being paid to talk, to lecture has brought to the very act of talking about ideas a spirit of violation, so that the joy of conversing is denied.

Stuart: I was saying before that the fifties and sixties facilitated certain kinds of conversations, but I also think that it may have to do with one's stage in life. I don't know that I have many conversations like that. There is a limited range of people with whom I have those sorts of conversations with now. This may have to do with what you were talking about earlier, that teaching, being paid to teach, is a way of being paid to talk, and so the status of talk is changed by that fact.

bell: I was thinking about the conditions under which Cornel West and I did *Breaking Bread*. I remember that we would meet in New York or he would come to Oberlin, Ohio at different times. There we would actually walk around this little town of cornfields and sing songs to each other, sit with our whiskey in the night, and I can't imagine doing that with him now. I hardly see him. When we talk it's talk on the run, not that talk amidst languorous times. I remember that there were several estate sales that we stopped to look at, and I think about how all of those things changed the nature of how we talked about ideas.

Stuart: It is as much about rhythm as anything else. If you are living the rest of your life at a certain intensified rhythm, it just doesn't fit the rhythm of conversation. You can't hurry. There has to be a certain space around conversation to allow it to either come or go, to last a short time or a long time, or to organize around established chunks.

bell: My early books were thought through in conversation, because I was in that liminal space between academy and a work world. When I was writing *Ain't I A Woman* and working 40 hours a week at the phone company there was this sense that if I had an idea that was the place I could go to test it out. There could be this ongoing conversation, and my sense of the book actually emerged as I talked it through with other people, and not as an internal, silent dialogue with myself.

Stuart: I don't think about writing like that. I think about thinking like that. So in that sense, I always, over any sustained period, work best intellectually with a group of people that is involved, and therefore, constantly talking in one form or another over our ideas. Writing is for me a much more isolated thing, but that is not to say that there isn't a conscious adoption of what might be called the conversational voice. In my writing I am more aware of speaking what I am saying than of writing it. When I write only, I write in a very clotted way, but as soon as I think about writing as I would speak it, I write in a much more accessible, vernacular way. There is a trace of conversation in spite of the fact that it hasn't actually come out of talking with others.

bell: A lot of people have characterized my work as having that conversational element, and in my case that is precisely right, because it does come out of daily conversations. I just finished a new book of essays on film and one of the essays came from going with a friend to see *Pulp Fiction*. We left the theater at midnight. After an intense, impassioned conversation about the movie, I went home, I wrote all night long. I wanted the writing to have the freshness and intensity of that conversation. If too much time goes by between my seeing a film, talking about it and then I'm not able to bring that intensity to the writing.

Stuart: I don't think of writing like that. For instance, I don't like to talk about films immediately after I see them. I get annoyed with people who instantly want to tell me what it's like. I want the film, the images to settle. In this sense, writing is for me an internal conversation. This is not to say that it doesn't make me look at it in restrospect, to see the trace of all those conversations that have happened before and come back into the writing. I don't think of writing as capturing conversation.

Conversation has to do with people. It is partly related to friendships and who one has around one. Here I am strangely placed, because I am out of my generation. The people I feel closest to now, whom I have conversations with, are a different generation from the generation I grew up in. I've left the generation I grew up with emotionally, and certainly intellectually and politically. I feel I was reborn in another time. It really is quite strange to discover that people can no longer imagine how old you are. I see this when I say that I have been around a very long time, and people often ask if I am from the sixties. I tell them, "No, the fifties!" I had very intense relationships with people in the fifties. They were older than I was which takes me back further. These were people born after the war in the forties, and that whole generation has not been present to me for about twenty to twenty-five years. This means that the people I am in conversation with are much younger than me, and it is not just a question of age, but more that their experience is very different. That is what I want. I am not complaining, but it does alter the nature of the conversation. The conversation is more like teaching. It has that character of the older person and the student, although they're teaching, and I'm learning.

bell: We have mentioned to each other many times that it was Paul Gilroy that kept saying to me, "The two of you need to talk." I kept saying to him, "but you know, I'm intimidated." I got scared, and you just touched upon why. Normally I am talking to people who are much younger than me or are colleagues and friends my age. Intergenerational dialogues don't really occur very often. I wonder how much that absence diminishes us. I remember Toni Cade Bambara telling me once that at some point in her life she looked around and found that she was only talking to people that were younger than her. She did not think this was good for her intellectual as well as her emotional development. She felt that she needed to have a range of peers. The fact that she was always dialoguing with younger audiences made her think about the relationship between conversation and power. "How will I talk to Stuart? Will I imagine that I am his peer?" It is interesting to think about the space that allows conversation to happen.

Stuart: I understand how she felt; although, I don't know that I have felt it myself in that way. I don't know that I could do anything about the constancy of intergenerational conversation in my life because of two transitions in my life. One is coming to England at the end of my youth, the beginning of my adulthood, and this does mean that there is already one generation that I have lost, the generation I was schooled with, the generation of my teenage life. All of that is lost. I don't mean that I don't know them. I see them when I go back to Jamaica, but their experience in the sixties and seventies was so profound, and so profoundly different than mine, which was also profound. It is two different experiences. They are not my interlocutors anymore. Thinking back that is one direction it went, and then there is another one, which is the one that I found when I came here, which I talked about, the one at the university involved in the New Left. I made a huge shift from that at some point in the sixties. At some point in the sixties I became again a very different person. Again, those people I know and know very well, and some of those people I still feel very close to, but some of them I don't feel that close to and haven't for quite a long time. I feel that with some of them I couldn't even have a conversation now, because they haven't a clue as to who I am.

bell: I have felt that most deeply within the feminist movement. I have continued to try to stretch myself while a lot of the people that I initially started out talking with in the early seventies haven't continued to want to stretch the meaning of feminism, the boundaries of feminism. In fact, there is a movement away from that stretching. The leap into cultural studies happened as a way to save myself from that static momentum, that conversation that had somewhat stopped.

Stuart: Unlike you when I talk about a political generation I am talking about a political generation that is enormously productive at liberating for a time, but which one comes to the generational end of, partly because everybody has died. It ceases to sustain you, because it doesn't move with you. When you talk about cultural studies as being a way of extending the boundaries, I understand, because it was for me too. So when I say "the sixties" I'm thinking everything that the sixties means politically, but I also mean cultural studies. And I mean communism particularly. That is part of what profoundly made me a different kind of person. Now what is interesting about that is that it gave me a new look which is the first feminist generation of the sixties and seventies. This is Catherine's generation, and she is much younger than I am, thirteen years younger than I am.

bell: My students were really obsessed with your discussion of cultural studies and feminism breaking through the window, and they were particularly disturbed by your use of the imagery of shit.

Stuart: Crap.

bell: Yes.

Stuart: So were the people in England. I didn't think of it like that. I thought of it as an old phrase: "Don't crap on the coffee table." Meaning, don't go to a polite place and make an impolite observation. I meant it more in that way, but of course who knows what unconsciously one means. For me, you might say there was a lot of shit associated with it, and there was, but I really didn't mean it that way. That is what feminism did, what feminism had to do.

bell: It had to create a rupture.

Stuart: Absolutely. It had to come into a conversation that had conceived of itself as rupturing. This was the progressive center, left wing, Marxist, committed scholarship inside the university, etc., and in the center of that conversation it had to do its own disruptive work.

bell: It is interesting though, because there are very few things that I've said that I feel regret about. In an interview last year in *Vibe* magazine I said that Oprah Winfrey was too busy sucking the dicks of white culture to get on with anything interesting, and people held me accountable for that statement as though it was a form of sexual violation in itself. I was stunned, because I didn't see it as a particularly risqué or outrageous thing to say. I didn't think of it as a particularly transgressive statement in any way. That is part of what has led to a certain kind of collapse within feminism, this desire to restrict the boundaries of how we talk about certain things, a certain kind of overlay of heavy-handed political correctness.

Stuart: It has happened to me one or two times before. Once when I was making *Redemption Song* and filming in Guyana. We went to Guyana principally to make the story of indenture.

It turned out to be a situation where there were many more polarized relationships between Indians and blacks than most people outside of Guyana either knew or would acknowledge was the case. While filming, these young Indian hair cutters said vile things about African Guyanese. We left in one of these statements simply because when we came to it we thought, "We don't like it, but this is what they feel." We felt that the program needed to communicate that they feel extremely oppressed by a black government. So we left in one of these statements. It has generated an enormous storm from the Caribbean. I went to a Guyanese restaurant a month ago, and remember we did the program two and a half years ago, and they still remember the statement: "We work hard and blacks just treat us like dogs." There were hundreds of statements like this, but we dropped this one in because we wondered what we would be doing if we censored all of them out, because we didn't want to air it. I don't have those sorts of feelings about what I said about feminism. I was caught in a time warp. I think the phrase, "crapping on the coffee table," is an old fifties idiom that I picked up from some American friends which nobody really knows. I shouldn't really have used it, but this is not to deny what you are saying about political correctness. It is a very serious problem for feminism to negotiate.

bell: Would you talk a little bit about the intersection of both your intellectual work at that particular point where feminism comes in and your private life as you are constructing a relationship with a feminist thinker? I feel that the men who were most changed by feminism were the men who had this joint convergence of the public, intellectual life of feminism, and also a private life of feminist interrogation. Especially when I think about men on the Left and look at the history of the Left. For instance, someone like Cornel who has not had, in the space of his private relationships, an ongoing exchange with a feminist partner who is constantly on you. I definitely think that any feminist woman partner that anybody has, man or woman, is usually on the case all the time.

Stuart: Absolutely. I certainly feel that you are right about the intersection of the public intellectual and the private. I hadn't thought that that's the impact that has the greatest effect, although that might be so.

bell: Once the mood of that particular moment, the moment feminism is entering through the window and working as an intervention, once that moment of militancy passed then it was possible for a lot of men to go back to a space and a location where they didn't think about feminism. The men who remained fully and deeply engaged on an emotional and intellectual level with feminist thinking in their private lives, as well as in their public lives, were not able to do that kind of backtracking.

Stuart: It happened the private, public way around for me. I went to Birmingham in 1964. Catherine and I were just married, and she was still a student. She transferred from Sussex to Birmingham. I was a young teacher involved in the Center, and she was a student studying history. Then in 1968 we moved, and she got pregnant. She was pregnant during the big '68 occupation of the University. One of the things I remember is seeing her in this great hall sitting down about two months from delivering Becky. It was immediately in the wake of that that feminism in Birmingham started, because all of these women, many of them University wives who had lead a very active life studying and organizing, had their first children in these two years and suddenly all retired to home. They found themselves with one baby sitting at home. That is where it started as they got together to share this incomprehension that this ball had descended from the blue. One moment she was getting her Ph.D., and then suddenly she had only the status of my wife. I would go to work. The Center burgeoned on, and I came back with stories of life at the front. That is when the explosion started. So it was very, very personal, tied up with our first child, and it made a profound shift in our relationship. Talk about shit, it was hell on earth, and partly exaggerated by the age difference. It wasn't just that I was a man, but I was a man fourteen years older that she was, already politically mature, with a political life, with friends she didn't know. You can just imagine what it was like for her to fight this off. It was a fight.

I shared the domestic work, that didn't bother me. I was into the familiar things, taking care of the home and looking after the kids, but the idea that I should shut up, that I should stop talking, that we should all stop talking for about twenty years, and let them talk was very, very difficult. It shifted my perception of politics, and I may get arrested for saying this, but it shifted my conception of politics more than it shifted some women's. Many of the women from that generation became Marxist feminists and have remained more in touch with Marxism than I have. I was more shaken by feminism's critique of Marxism than they were. Subsequently, I find myself saying, "You can't say that. You told us how feminism made what you are saying impossible. I don't understand."

bell: That is a really good point. It leads us back to a critique of feminism and essentialism. Simply because one is a woman and has laid claim to feminism does not mean that you are necessarily more transformed by it as a political movement and a body of ideas than any man who engages that body of ideas.

Stuart: That is at any rate an indication that it was enormously profound, of course for them, but it was extremely profound for me in terms of shaking what I thought I knew and what I thought I believed. Consequently, those women are some of my closest friends now. It opened a conversation with many sixties and seventies generation feminists.

bell: Were there very many black women involved in there, Stuart? A critique that I often get when I am speaking about the various intellectual and critical dialogues that I have had with you, and for instance, Paul Gilroy, from black women in Britain is, "They'll talk to you, because you live in America. But they won't talk to us. They don't recognize us."

Stuart: That may be true. Who am I to say? Historically, there weren't a lot of black women involved at that time, very few. My experience of what has happened in that particular formation is, first of all, it was raced as the black women came into it. And then, what in many ways has been most impressive to me, are the few white feminists who, as a consequence of black women entering the movement, have rethought themselves a second time.

bell: Absolutely.

Stuart: All of that is very profound. This was the sequence of events so I am not surprised that in the sixties in Birmingham there weren't many black women around. Therefore, I wasn't in conversation with black women. Then when black women come into feminism it is a generation later.

bell: The dialogue we had at the Finding Fanon Conference at NYU was emblematic of these different positions, in the sense that I wanted to privilege, in my own discussion, a certain kind of dialogue between black men and black women. Not the traditional discussion of relationships, but of gender and feminism. In a different way than white women involved in feminism might pose that particular dialogue.

Stuart: But also, bell, in a different way than some black women would pose that particular dialogue.

bell: Absolutely, although there is a way in which many black women thinkers in Britain have retreated from the spheres of public debate. One of the things that I was very cognizant of in that space was that there were powerful black women thinkers there, but they were not speaking. I believe, to some extent, that that retreat is about who listens. This does have to do with questions of kinship and history. Thinking about my intimidation in speaking with you I am aware that there are white women feminist thinkers who could speak to you with a greater sense of comfort, but I do think, and you can critique me on this, this is partially because I see myself in a closer kinship to you. For example, when I taught my class on your work we were reading "The Formation of a Diasporic Intellectual," the interview you did with Kuan-Hsing Chen (1996), and when we came to the part about your sister, in a class of Afro-Caribbean, for the most part, all black women and one white woman, every black woman in that class, including myself, felt that we were your sister, and that her fate was our fate, in a way that the one white student in the class did not feel.

Stuart: I understand that perfectly well. It is difficult to transfer that to the wider scene. It is because race is so intrinsic to that experience.

bell: But in terms of speaking, of feeling that you can speak back to something, that sense of interrogation comes sometimes with feeling that you are the closer kin. It becomes a symbolic family bond, in the sense that it has been historically more difficult for black women to bring a feminist critique to bear without thinking about what the implications are in terms of racial identity and racial solidarity. We have been working to overcome that intimidation. In many ways I never felt that intimidation, and I think it is generational again. Part of what separates me from some of the older black women Marxist feminists is that I was a young student in the seventies. I came into Marxist thinking from feminism, and that is an altogether different location of power and of voice.

Stuart: Those generational questions are very seriously neglected.

bell: A lot of those black women thinkers resent people like myself, a person who could say that comment about Oprah Winfrey and not think it was a charged negation of her. It was in fact that older generation of feminists that felt it was a violent put down and a mockery of sisterhood. I saw it as hard hitting critique.

Stuart: There are those generational differences, and the story in relation to the Center is also important in this context. Having begun to be transformed by this feminist experience, once one found a voice, a different voice, within the conversations that were going on within the feminist movement in Birmingham at the time, the question was, "What impact is that going to have on cultural studies?" My memory of it, although it is sometimes contested in its history and detail, is that two of us men at the Center who were living with feminists and who were involved in this maelstrom proposed that feminism should be introduced into the Center. You can imagine what a ridiculous notion this was that we were going to parachute feminism in. It didn't really take the first time. We wanted to bring in two outside writers to socialize feminist ideas. People were not particularly interested. They were not particularly feminists. They were not particularly involved. When feminism did come as an autonomous force we were the objects, inevitably, of another kind of public silencing which of course we felt deeply resentful about. The idea that we would try to stop them was a completely mistaken notion. Now I am not trying to defend the notion. I am trying to recreate the psychological view. We tried to get this thing in, and the women were not interested. Then, to be blamed for not responding when feminism descended was inevitable. The word was full of double moves like this. Misunderstandings were everywhere. That is what I meant by feminism crapping on the coffee table.

bell: Do you think that we now can understand more that that was part of the political process in the same way that black women trying to bring the discussion of race into feminism were perceived as another kind of crapping on the table? There was a ferociousness with which white women tried to silence me ten to twenty years ago, and yet now I can have an incredible sense of delight to see so many of those women using race as a part of reshaping their political imaginations and their actions. But at the time nobody wanted to hear it. The discourse of race is so permeated in feminist studies and cultural studies that people have already forgotten the incredible hostility at its introduction.

Stuart: I am sure you know from the work Paul has written that the same thing happened around race at the Center, exactly the same. Everyone is a good liberal, sensitive to questions of race, until a group wants to start that is going to study this, and then all hell breaks loose. Now that this is everywhere, including cultural studies, everyone has completely forgotten those resistances. There is more to be said about that. One facet of it is that when you are involved in that struggle you live it moment by moment in each of its contradictory forms, and you can't surmount that to see that this is part of a long struggle. Another aspect is, which is the aspect that interested me most about the Center, the nature of unconscious resistance. By then I had no conscious resistances at all. I was completely in favor of everything, but I had unconscious resistances. I wouldn't let certain texts be included in the lead provision in the M.A. I even had sophisticated reasons why the people, the men, who were already there were the ones who we all needed to study. It seemed perfectly logical to me. It had nothing to do with my feelings about feminism. The level of archaic feelings are for me now completely astonishing, but at the time they were very real. You have to appreciate that this was inside a Center that was trying to be more democratic, where against the grain, we had open discussions, had meetings and took votes that told teachers what to do. It was a very democratic place. Despite this, attempts were made within that democratization to reserve power by a certain kind of man, by a certain kind of masculine formation, and this tells you something about the level at which authority operates day by day which most people do not talk about. They don't talk about this level. This is the level at which it actually operates, unrolls from moment to moment, from one side to the other.

bell: What allows you to finally face that unconscious resistance? I believe that that is the tension that so many women active in feminist politics feel, particularly thinking of separatist feminists, that most men never reach the point where they interrogate that unconscious resistance.

Stuart: I was astonished to find it in myself, and I hated being put in that position. That is why I left the Center. I refused to be in the patriarchal position. There were only three teachers in the Center, and the rest of the people who made up the Center were graduate students. There was no other place to go but to the head, patriarchal, old leader. There was just no space to move. I realized that you couldn't be in that position and facilitate. I could never do it. They didn't want me to do it, and quite rightly they didn't want me to do it. They wanted to do it for themselves, but I couldn't stand that they had to do it for themselves against me when I didn't want to be in that space. So I lost the unconscious investment I had in that space and I had to get out. I left because it was just not possible for me to be in that position anymore. I stepped sideways into another version of myself, but I wasn't able to become another version of myself and maintain the structural position I had in the Center.

bell: That sense of displacement is exactly what many men continue to fear about feminism. It is that part of the process of decolonizing one's mind in terms of sexism that requires specific shifts in perspective.

Stuart: Of course it is. I knew that from the very first moment. I had resisted it personally, and then kind of came to terms with it. Then I thought I had moved it forward publicly, but then I really resisted it publicly. I had to come to terms with that. That resistance is certainly there all the way along.

bell: To conclude this, I want to return to the moment when all of us were thinking that we were your sister. Your sister was left at home, and you were able to move. I have been questioning symbolically why that touched us all so deeply. There is the sense that the black man is able to move in the diaspora, and the black female is trapped, is caught.

Stuart: That is the guilt of my life. I was determined to move. I knew I wanted to move. I said I wanted to move, but I didn't know it would be for good. Actually, unconsciously I was never going back, because I would be going back to her space, to that space which is a space that was prepared for all of us. All of us should have been where she was. She was in the hospital. All of us were meant to be there. But I got out, and she couldn't.

bell: It is interesting for me to think about this in terms also of what we were saying at the conference about Frantz Fanon not returning home. I do see it as a political project in the symbolic sense of home, both to have this conversation with you, this series of conversations, and the conversations that I had with Cornel, to create the notion of a feminist solidarity between black women and men existing on the level of the discourse of relationships, of personal relationships, trying to talk about the significance of that intellectual dialogue that allows us both to leave home.

Stuart: I understand that it would be that moment, because I understand that it would be a very representative experience for all of us, which is to say, that we are already not at home. It is all written in the stars that at some moment we should also leave where we have come to call home. Some people leave and some don't, and there is the impossibility then, or the difficulty of then building any kind of bridge back to what that was that isn't just a relationship about return, nostalgia, or romanticizing it. I feel an umbilical cord to the space of home, and yet I can't possibly have gone home. I feel both things as profoundly as ever. In a way I never left it. In another way I left it from the beginning, because I never felt that I belonged. I wanted to get out. What I watched happen to my sister at seventeen was part of the whole situation of our family, and it is not just our family because our family was representative of a whole class in a colonial culture, and I knew everything that had made her ill was designed to make all of us ill. I was already ill from it, but I knew if I stayed there I would die, not only emotionally, but spiritually. I knew I would completely perish.

bell: I was saying that it was feminism that allowed me to leave home, and part of why my intellectual focus has continued to bring feminism into the discourse of race, and into concrete politics of black life in the diaspora, has been because I feel that black women will never be able to leave home without it.

Stuart: Of course, it wasn't feminism that made me leave home. It was too early for that. It was race. Race in a very complicated way. It was race in the colonial setting, race inside my family, not black/white race, but the way in which my family had internalized race, and then used it as a way of categorizing the world. It was my awareness of race in that sense, and I never lost that notion of race as both a public structure and a psychic, personal experience. I just don't understand the separation that is sometimes made between these two things. My sister was psychologically, profoundly damaged by the racist nature of the colonial culture.

bell: But also, that that culture converged with gender politics.

Stuart: Yes, but I didn't understand that at the time. I left because of race, but it was afterwards that feminism made me understand why she couldn't leave and I could leave. That was a dimension that I didn't understand until much later on.

bell: Was that any kind of solace?

Stuart: No, it is no solace at all. It is compounded further. But it made me understand.

bell: I mean in the sense that it took away the personal implication, it should take away the sense that there was anything that you, personally, could have done.

Stuart: Yes, that is true.

bell: Why do you think, knowing what we know, it has been so difficult to continue to bring that feminist element into the discourses of race, particularly those that are coming from a black nationalist standpoint?

Stuart: I don't understand it really. I don't know why that is so, because as soon as you reflect very deeply on what race means in terms of the shaping of people's lives it breaks along gender lines immediately. I have never understood how you could see the one without somehow seeing the other, but it is clear that it is possible. Not only that, but there is a certain kind of political discourse which isn't able to handle that doubleness of the categories, the thinking in two ways which that way of understanding requires.

bell: It also goes back to the fact that that understanding cannot happen without a rupture. It then becomes a deconstruction and a breaking apart of what has come before that we then have to rebuild. I think that there have been a lot of black male political thinkers and public intellectuals that don't want to have to do the work. That is why I am still quite impressed by women in the feminist movement and those white women who were willing, in fact, to allow themselves to be transformed by that rupture. I still see feminism as an exemplary political movement on that particular terrain. I feel that many people don't want to see this about feminism. It wasn't like we just said the feminist movement is racist and left it there, but, in fact, there were these concrete ruptures that then lead to a rethinking of the direction of the movement. But it did create an enormous sense of loss for a lot of people who were nostalgic for that earlier version of feminism, and who remain nostalgic for that earlier version of feminism.

Stuart: Yes, and the resistances do come also from a certain nostalgia for an earlier form of life. At that level, the patriarchal nature of a great deal of black culture is a kind of compensation for all that is experienced in the oppression and subordination of race.

bell: That is what I would like our next discussion to be about, the notion of home and homecoming, because in order for us to move past this we have to reinvent the notion of home. As long as home is that nostalgic return to the patriarchal household then it can never allow feminism to come through the window or the door.

Stuart: It doesn't allow the rupture to reach those levels of disturbance which make people transform themselves and take on a transformed politics as well.

bell: I was thinking about Paul Gilroy talking about how black Americans seem to be particularly hung up on the idea of family as the only site of renewal which takes us back again and again to the patriarchal paradigm. We certainly saw that with Farrakhan and The Million Man March.

Stuart: I agree with what he says about that. Historically it is perfectly intelligible why that is so.

bell: Why?

Stuart: The constitution of the family itself under slavery was an act of resistance. It is so tied up with freedom, autonomy, and reclaiming control over your life. It obviously has a very powerful, positive resonance about it. Then there is the absence of the other structures. For instance, there has never been any kind of adequate national, political representation of black people. They are excluded from so many of the civil structures of society that inevitably the family is a kind of last refuge, the first refuge and the last refuge. It's not surprising, but nevertheless, it is a problem, a problem for us all. The Jamaican case is slightly different. The family is strongly valued. It's not something so ideologically pushed. It's more emotionally there. Actually, the family is the functioning unit which everybody is attached to and defending, and particularly men leave, move from one family to another, from their mother's family to their wives. They don't leave that emotionally until they move to their wives or their own constituency's family. This stepping from family to family is very important, especially among middle-class people. Amongst more popular communities where the position of women has been absolutely central, as you know, it is very much matrifocal, matrifocal but within a patriarchal dominant society. This split in Jamaica inside the black family itself, with women being the only binding and consistent force that has remained there, and yet, in a certain very important way sexually, quite often financially, in relation to the property, in relation to authority of the children having very little power. This double tension makes it a place to go back to, to resolve problems that may reconstitute something or other like that in the next generation. It is a real, deep problem particularly for post-slave plantation diaspora societies.

bell: You just hit upon a crucial misunderstanding. Certainly, as a feminist thinker in the last twenty years, the major problem I have in talking to diverse black communities is that people want to say, "We are completely woman dominated." To have people understand the difference between that matrifocal, yet still patriarchal base is always the one-hundred-dollar misunderstanding. It's still the primary dilemma around gender and race in the United States.

Stuart: I agree. Is it possible to understand masculinity without that double institution?

bell: Actually, that was my other choice of focus for these beginning conversations: masculinity, because that is where there has been the least reworking.

Stuart: That is true in practice. Again you can see exactly why, with emasculation being so central to the whole slave, and post-slave cultures, that the claiming of masculinity takes a certain form. What surprises me is that people who have been through that, even though they are psychologically and psychically formed by that experience, can't stand sufficiently outside of it to understand the way in which they reenact the drama outside and inside the space of the family. That has been a consistent temptation and tendency.

bell: That is why the work of black gay male theorists has been so important, because globally they appear to be that group of people, in terms of black masculinity and masculinity in general, that have been willing to stand outside. Largely because, on one level, the very fact of homosexuality means that they're always outside to begin with.

Stuart: Yes, they simply cannot recapitulate the battle, because they are already outside of it so that they have a way into it which comes at it from a different angle. Also, very substantially, and again historically one can understand why, but because this is so tied up with the body. The fact is that a lot of that work by black gay theorists has taken the form of visual work, of film, of painting, of the use of imagery, of attention to the black body. The refiguring of the black body is so important that it actually is the only way of getting past some of the constructions that have been put in place, through to where the complexities of the feelings are where this double inscription really operates.

bell: But once again, we saw at the Fanon conference in the discussion about the portrayal of sodomy in Raoul Peck's film, *The Man by the Shore*, this complete unwillingness on the part of "the straight mind," to use Monique Wittig's phrase, to comprehend what was being presented. We were seeing the straight mind in action when audiences could not conceptualize the vital signification of that particular moment in the film.

Stuart: I thought it was a riveting moment. I like Raoul Peck very much as a person. I respect his work. I thought the film was very powerful. I thought that scene was very powerful, and yet, when he came to talk about it, it was as if he could not see what he himself had put into motion. I do agree with you.

bell: It is making me wonder then how, if underlying the inability of black masculinity to make a break with patriarchy is the overwhelming fear of homosexuality how then can we intervene in any way? One of the major interventions has been against the prevailing assumption that if we in any way affirm diverse sexual practices we are denying the black family. Most people don't want to acknowledge that most black gays and lesbians, particularly if they are over 30, usually have come out of traditional marriages, and usually have children. There is a myth of black gayness being anti-family, because black gayness has not constituted itself in the ways of the norm which white gayness has constituted itself upon.

Stuart: Or that white gayness is trying to constitute itself as. That is true, but in some ways this should take us back, not just to the question of masculinity and the challenge of gay black masculinity, to the masculine norms, but to the family itself. It is a very particular image of the family that sets itself up as inevitably, and in all instances, opposed by the fact of sexual diversity. It is because we think that the family requires a certain kind of sexual monogamy, and a certain kind of prescription of sexual identities. All of that other stuff is loaded onto the image of the family, but then we get a polarization. You are either in this camp, or in that camp. Whereas, the wider context is really trying to rethink, to relive, to reconfigure all of those relationships across the spectrum. The persistence of sexual jealousy within the monogamous, heterosexual family, is itself a problem. It's a problem for the family. It's a problem for not only those who break it, it's a problem for the family itself, because it very often maintains and requires all kinds of falsifications in order to preserve it intact. There are many other roots to families living together which can accept a much wider diversity of practices throughout people's lives, at different stages of people's lives. This includes the notion that marriage is continually renegotiated, including the sexual dimension. It is not just the alternative forms. It is inside the dominant form. It is our image of the dominant form itself which is so unyielding, and which has, for certain good reasons, been, with certain differences, recapitulated inside of black culture in a subordinate position that holds the whole structure together. In a sense, a heterosexual matrix operates and inscribes both those inside it and outside it. That is really a profound area where questions of gender and sexuality, and questions of race come together.

bell: That has been one of my major areas of disagreement with Paul Gilroy, because I don't feel that the idea of family, in and of itself, is necessarily only a conservative and reactive site. I believe it is our inability to expand the concept of family. The family remains a location of self-determination. For instance, part of why Harriet Tubman starts a school in her house, in her living room, part of why so much civil rights activism starts in the living room or the kitchen, is because those are the spaces, finally, that people have some control over. In grappling with domestic space and family, my question is why such a conservative vision of the family has prevailed. I just finished writing a piece about my grandparents who were married for seventy some years, and how when I was growing up I didn't know any of these older black couples who shared rooms. I had no concept that you were going to grow up, marry somebody, and sleep in the same room with them for seventy-some-years. They each had their separate rooms with their separate kinds of personalities. It is what I call continually "the oppositional world view" that nobody really wants to look at. People don't really want to see how much racial integration, and the desire to assimilate to a bourgeois norm truly altered the family as it had previously been conceived in its diversity. For many of us growing up in the apartheid South, in my own small southern community there were prominent gay black men who adopted children, who lived with men, but who daily visited their real families and their real parents. It was about class power and care. I have talked with other black people who come from small Southern communities who found the same inter-being, inter-locking structures of community and family. By not paying attention to, by not valorizing, by simply going toward the heterosexist norm we deny the beauty of our own diversity in our historical past which, to me, is important to try to name and recover in an effort to say, "It's not the family that is the problem, it's the heterosexist paradigm."

Stuart: It's interesting what you say. It's not quite the same in the Jamaican context, but in some ways it is. There is very much a class divide, and of course, amongst ordinary working people, especially outside of Kingston, outside of the big city, families and communities are very closely intertwined. People have a much wider diversity of kinship; some are parts of real families or symbolic associations between families. There is, in fact, a diversity of relationships going on which are very far from the nuclear family as the norm. Where that begins to enter is, of course, in the educated, middle class for whom the very notion of social mobility is mobility towards that enclosed reconstituted family domain.

bell: In my own critique of The Million Man March what I have found to be most difficult as I went around the states was the willingness on people's part to acknowledge that this march was about class and class values. That it wasn't a reclamation of the family. It was a reclamation of a particular view of family life. What I was amazed by was people's absolute refusal to want to see class. What I see happening in the United States, and I know you see it happening here as well, is that so many families without money have no notion that grown children will live apart from their parents. In fact, what most studies are showing, especially among all groups of people, across race, who don't have a lot of money, is that the notion that mom and dad will get to be sixty and have the house to themselves is completely false, is completely gone. Now at varied intervals children are coming back so that the notion of a privatized nuclear family is completely disrupted by the reality of those kinds of movements. For instance, people like my siblings who have been drug addicts and who when they are drug addicted abandon their children. Then, in turn, the children have to be taken in by the grandparents, or aunts and uncles. Then they become sober again at some point and different shifts occur.

The flexibility of the family and its ability to sustain itself without patriarchal foundation is to me the big secret. No one wants to look at the resiliency of community and family outside the context of patriarchy. It is almost a mockery of this for Farrakhan and others to act as though the family—

Stuart:—is this one norm or nothing.

bell: Yes, and that that can sustain us in a moment of crisis. I was thinking about you and Paul Gilroy, and wondering if part of our dilemma around the critique of patriarchy and black masculinity is that so many brilliant black male thinkers are perceived as not a part of something we call the black family. They have married, for example, interracially. Their views on family, in a sense, are not listened to. I have been trying to think, "How then can we make that shift?" I was thinking about Fanon, and how people listen to Fanon up to a point, but then that point when they feel like we begin to talk about masculinity and the family—

Stuart:—at that point he stops having something to say, or people stop listening to him. I dare suppose that in my own case I would have said that the important thing was not the fact of interracial marriage, because left to myself I could well have tried to recapitulate that norm inside my own family. If I think about Jamaican middle-class society, which isn't interracial in terms of black and white, but which is in the internal color race system. Interracially, it very often consists of much blacker men with much fairer middle-class women so it is not uninscribed by the racial insignia. They reproduce this norm perfectly. It is not only race, it has to do with other things. In my own instance, it was feminism that disrupted the terms on which I first got married. We all collude in traditional ways to be married that are completely different from the way in which we have had to go on. After getting married the old model was completely impossible, either we weren't going to take the critique of patriarchy into our emotional life or we had to find a completely different way of living together. I'm not suggesting it is easy or that I have done it. I am just saying that what disrupts it is not just the racial question. It is sometimes put to me like that. Just recently someone asked me to participate in a program they want to do on interracial marriage. It is beginning to be a question again, a question of interracial marriage in Britain. It surfaces now and again. I said no to them, because I don't think they are going to ask me the right question. They are going to assume because I married a white woman this in itself must represent the entry into some completely unknown space which is unintelligible in terms of the way it is structured. I don't think this is true anymore.

bell: In the United States many of the progressive black male intellectuals and thinkers on the left have not tended to bond romantically with partners who are engaged in the feminist movement. On the one hand, here are these men who stand up and speak against sexism, but they are not any different from Jesse Jackson or other people in that we never see their wives, we never hear their wives, we don't know anything about what they do. I was trying to think about what is different in the British context so that if we were to write down our black male thinkers, whether their partners are white, black, brown or what have you, you have much more of a kind of peer bonding around shared political perspectives, activism, and intellectual activity, opposed to a more traditional norm. I have wondered whether that deeply affects the inability of us to ground new thinking about black liberation in feminist thought in the States. I really felt that Cornel West's support of The Million Man March was a tremendous political regression, because he has been so much the symbol of progressive black masculinity. It was as though he was coming out in affirmation of the patriarchal, heterosexist family model. That was very distressing to me.

Stuart: Yes. You know I hadn't thought about that difference between America and England, although, I think that you are probably right. At some point we need to talk about the difference in the two societies, in how race figures in the two societies. I think it is very different for some complicated reasons. I must say in my own instance it is unfortunately not that I made that positive choice, because this hit us, as it were, after I made the choice. The contract was made.

bell: What I have heard, Stuart, is that you have always been attracted to women of power, who are creative.

Stuart: That is certainly true. There were always shared political and intellectual perspectives. I was just pointing out that feminism, specifically, was something that, as it were, came into the middle of our relationship. You are quite right. That is probably true about England. I hadn't thought about that.

bell: I really wonder to what extent black women thinkers engaged with feminism early on were not able to intervene in that the majority of those thinkers were and remain lesbian women, in terms of the prominent, powerful thinkers within the movement. I looked up one day and saw that I was one of the few prominent black women feminist thinkers that still had any engagement with men at all. While, not to engage a kind of essentialism, I thought that we have to have the actual practice of a feminist black heterosexuality if we are ever going to convince people that it is necessary to intervene. This is what I was trying to bring to the table at the Fanon Conference that I perhaps didn't do skillfully enough, but I was trying to say that there has to be some recognition of the need for a feminist dialogue that can take place between black men and women that is not about erotic relationships, but is about meeting each other as two subjects.

Stuart: I am sure that is essential. In a way it has been a missing dimension in the more effective conversations that have been connected around that space, a space that has been weakly occupied. Don't you think this is, as you said before, because questions of masculinity are more easily posed by black gay men. They are structurally outside, and consequently, see life differently. In some ways I think that's also true of relationships between heterosexual men and heterosexual women. That is to say that the very nature of the heterosexual matrix holds that conversation in a way, within such powerful models, that it is quite difficult to remain inside, strongly inside that, as an erotic position, and at the same time to question or interrogate how it works. How the relationship works itself out across a period of time for instance. How it is sustained across time.

bell: It is interesting that at the point when I meet Paul Gilroy it is the moment when his students are using my work to bring a powerful critique to his work around the question of race and feminism. This question has been in my dialogues with men of color from other countries, such as Paul or for instance Paulo Freire from Brazil. These men have been more open to having their work transformed by feminist thinking, their own feminist thinking and that of the women they read, more so than African American male intellectuals. To some extent the rise of the black intellectual in the United States has coincided with the notion of the intellectual as a father patriarch so that the lead men such as Henry Louis Gates, Cornel West and different men become symbolic of the restoration of the lost father patriarchy.

That is why I think we see those men having a much fiercer critique of sexism earlier on in their careers and less so as they become public symbols of a renewed black intellectual spirit.

Stuart: This conversation would be very different if it was conducted in Britain across class lines. If you were talking to young black men with a working class background involved in the music industry, or something like that, they would not really know what you were talking about. In that space, I am afraid to say, these young men are very influenced by the American model. The American model has become, over about ten years, amongst that kind of conscious, but non-intellectual in terms of the work they do, young black man, a very powerful model which is one of the reasons why black music here has gone back to a strong affirmation of patriarchal, homophobic thinking. It is very tied into that culture. We are really talking across the intellectual, class divide. As far as this is concerned the interracial question might indeed have an important role to play.

bell: I agree.

Stuart: The liaison with certain white women moves them to encounter feminism at a very early stage, and the critique that has brought a lot of black women into feminism comes in Britain at a later stage than that. Therefore, by the time that happens black men are already so in their making of relationships with women they can't quite make it in the ways in which they used to be able to. They bring into the relationships in which they might then form with other black women a recognition that these are going to be intellectual women, women with a stronger sense of their own position, with a politics of their own, that they are going to be people who want to establish a relationship across a critique, not on the basis that I will never critique men, the idea that now that we are partners I will never say anything against you is going to be more con-tested, more argued, more negotiating for position. We are all already entering relationships knowing that they are going to be like that before they actually happen to us.

bell: When we think about the historical development of contempo-rary American feminism, in fact, sexism is being questioned within the context of black nationalist movement, and there is not that conver-gence of black men with those white women who are strongly engag-ing feminist thinking in the same way. For instance, when we read a book like Sara Evans' *Personal Politics* (1979) on white women in the civil rights struggle we see the rhetoric of subordination to the greater cause of racial freedom supersedes the convergence of feminism and black liberation. They then become parallel movements that are in fact presented as at odds with each other which is why I think it takes this younger generation of black women, people like myself, who were actually entering college at the height of contemporary feminism, who then become the people who move away from the notion of questioning sexism within nationalism, because in fact we are questioning the whole system, the family, the notion of nation. I was coming out of a context of free love, not at all the traditional context for black politicization.

Stuart: It has a lot to do with the fact that black politicization, black political culture, themselves were so underpinned by a whole substructure of relations around sexuality and gender that were not open to inspection.

bell: There is also a frightening way that stars are constructed in black political culture. For instance, I don't think many people remember that Angela Davis was not someone who came to the forefront as a feminist, that in fact, what brought her into public view was her subordinated presence in relationship to the thinking black man, and in George Jackson's case, the figure of a working class rebellion. It was all of masculinity. It was the black female intellectual in the service of this potent, powerful, heterosexual black masculinity. Part of the sadness of people not going back to *Blood in My Eye* is that when you read it you see how deeply misogynist and heterosexist it is in its visioning of revolution. It charts through generations the development of someone like Angela Davis, and people have to acknowledge that she comes to claim feminism much later in her political development.

Stuart: Of course, and that enables a critique or review of the earlier period which she couldn't have made without this experience.

bell: The person whose career, in terms of the development of feminist thinking, that stands out is Audre Lorde. Audre Lorde's politicization happens with an acknowledged convergence of race, sex and class.

Stuart: Yes, this is very distinctive.

bell: As a poet people have not tended to valorize her work as political.

Stuart: They quote her for the experience that she records but not for the ideas that are implicit in the experiences that she is recording which is often how knowledge gets distorted when it appears in another aesthetic form.

bell: In the documentary *Litany for Survival* part of what it depicts is that she is politicized within the context of literacy struggles and voting right struggles in the South, that she is not separate from those struggles coming into the politicization of herself as a lesbian.

Stuart: She has a very distinctive voice in which all of those things can be reflected simultaneously, rather than sequentially.

bell: It is a tremendous dilemma. Lorraine Hansberry is another central model for me of a public intellectual whose political involvement with Africa and Ethiopia in particular is forgotten. The irony is that as she becomes more and more claimed as a lesbian icon people pay less and less attention to how progressive she was on so many different fronts. This is what intrigues me about her. She raised early on the question of love and oppression asking if there could really be love in black families. Hansberry was one of the first people to say, "I don't find the kind of warmth among black people that the stereotypes would have us believe. I find a real tragic woundedness." Those aspects of her thinking have yet to be really remembered. I often question how much this has to do with the fact that the recorders of our history primarily remain the patriarchal straight mind, and that it is very convenient for that mind to ignore that there were women who were much more prophetic in what they were thinking about. A lot of the contemporary black male thinkers address certain things as though they—

Stuart:—As though they had only just thought it.

bell: And really women such as Hansberry had been formulating these ideas some time earlier. Amy Garvey is another person whose thoughts and works do not get attention even though she was really pushing Marcus Garvey to think more deeply about gender.

Stuart: That is absolutely true. Also, it is not a willful neglect, it is more an inability to see into the complexity of intellectual and political formation that is going on. Men think that women must come to these insights along a given, rather straightforward emotional feminized root, and so they don't look at these careers in the way in which they would look at the complexity of masculine careers as if they were very deep, having many ruptures, phases and evolutions. We don't get accounts of the politicization of women which take those complex histories into account, and consequently the prophetic insides of a lot of women's work are lost, because people don't see quite how original they were.

bell: One of the things that I have been trying to document is my own very deep involvement with the beat poets and the beat generation, to try to say that, in fact, the things that were influencing me when I was eighteen and nineteen years old writing *Ain't I A Woman* were really not solely the world of the segregated black southern experience that I came out of, but my obsessive interest in sexual liberation, free love, the beat poets and what they were doing with Buddhism, as well as other things. I have only recently begun to think that it's important to document those movements so that the essentialist framework of black intellectual development is not just reaffirmed again and again. One of the major concerns that I have had with my students, particularly with the resurgence of a narrow black nationalism, is their feeling that they don't have to read or study anything that is not coming out of an Afro-centric base. This is a good point to segue into a discussion of black intellectual life. Is it happening here in Britain with the same force that it is happening in the states in terms of Afrocentrism?

Stuart: It is not happening with the same force, but it is a continuing current. As I said earlier on, it is a stronger current outside of intellectual circles, but it has a sort of impact on intellectual circles as well, as you can imagine. But even when you don't have black intellectuals who would put a simple Afrocentric, essentialist framework on things, you do have a general assumption in the culture that black intellectuals must be formed by black things, and address only black questions. It is an extraordinary narrowing which has gone on. I have always had a particular strategic approach to this. It has always come out of the fact that, particularly in Britain where in spite of the long imperial connection, etc., a black presence in large numbers is relatively recent. It is very confined and constrained in terms of its disposition across this site as a whole to speak always as articulating on behalf of an interest group only that which the interest group can take any serious interest in as if these questions don't really relate to the rest of society at all. What happens about blackness doesn't affect them at all. It just affects us, and our rights, and our beings. I have always found that a false position to be in as an intellectual, and I have insisted that I try and find a way of addressing these questions that makes it as essential to them as it is to us.

bell: It is an irony of contemporary narrow nationalism that growing up in the context of racial apartheid and being educated in that context no one doubted whether or not we could speak French or whether we could learn German, because it was just assumed that we could do those things. The whole context of the world in which we were educated was that we were being educated to be thinkers in the world. The irony is that this education is taking place in the context of segregation, and it's all black. The sense of the intellectual is of an ambassador to the world. It was very limiting for me when they integrated the schools, and suddenly people were seeing me solely in relationship to race. I was not accustomed to seeing myself only in that way. When I stood up in my gymnasium in my all black school to recite Wordsworth the assumption was that all of the students sitting there had something at stake in Wordsworth. This has been a real dilemma.

Stuart: That is the real narrowing of an essentialist politics.

bell: And it has been a narrowing that has taken place on both sides in America, on the side of white people saying, "You can be among us as long as you stay—

Stuart:—a voice for your people."

bell: And on the side of black people now saying,—

Stuart:—"You can only be authentic if you are the voice of our people." Those two things play into one another, and they play in very strongly.

bell: Clearly, they inhibit the development of black intellectual thought. Part of the significance of Paul Gilroy's *The Black Atlantic* was its reminder to people that individuals like Richard Wright, James Weldon Johnson and W.E.B. Du Bois were moving around the world and engaged in a diasporic dialogue.

Stuart: That is one of the most important things about that book. It makes those lateral connections to the rest of the world. It breaks the confinement which an essentialist politics or perspective puts on these figures. For myself that is what the diasporic means. It means someone has to always be in conversation across geographical, spatial, intellectual segregated boundaries, otherwise there couldn't be a formation of a black intellectual class at all. The black political perspective that wasn't deformed by exactly the experiences of trying to get the measurer out. The place, it has to have a wider perspective. They are quite right in the sense that those intellectual boundaries continue to be racially inscribed, and that you don't just float across them like a bee and sit where you like.

bell: That is why I felt that I had a lot to offer in the sense that I wasn't coming out of a context of unloving blackness. That in fact I was coming out of a total context of blackness when I went to Stanford from that segregated black world. I have seen as central to my political project as a feminist thinker, and in terms of intellectual work around race and being, a presence that says you can love blackness and simultaneously have this expansive interest in many other things.

Stuart: Yes. That is the combination which one has to try to give political meaning. That is the problem where I think we come up against the barriers. That's why we can carry that idea forward more powerfully, because it has always been difficult to find a politics which is adequate to that view. So constantly the politics drive us back either to deserting our side, to becoming a voice of the world and inscribing someone else's agenda, or speaking from within and consequently being confined to it. This is why more advances seem to be made on the intellectual, artistic, and aesthetic front than can be made on the political. It is as if the political hangs behind some of the things that we are now able to see and speak of intellectually. Again *The Black Atlantic* is so important in giving, in a vivid and profound way, continual evidence of this in relation to some of the major figures of the whole movement historically.

bell: Where the book becomes problematic is that it is not able to frame that relation to a progressive politics for the future. It's exactly what you just stated. We can do it in the realm of art. We can do it in the realm of music and writing, but when it comes to envisioning what this expansive politics would look like it becomes very difficult.

Stuart: It does become difficult, and the book does not succeed in doing that. One has to ask which book could or does snatch this out of the air. There are attempts to do this in the way that music is written about in the end. It is a metaphor for this, of the changing same and how that concept is applied to the domain of the aesthetic in black popular culture. This is what stands in the book in place of any more grounded way of sketching a politics adequate to the intellectual position it has. It's a metaphor since we don't have anything else. I turn to this question because in relation to some of the more celebratory diasporic forms, both of politics and intellectual work, I'm sometimes seen as hanging back a bit with the essentialists, in retaining an interest in speaking within the black position. There are two reasons for this, one is the one that you have given, which is that one always speaks out of a particular space, or spaces, out of a site, out of particular languages, and you are going to love, and respect, and honor those languages that have allowed you to speak at all, which enable you to speak at all. Everybody comes from somewhere. They don't just come from the world, they come from somewhere, and address the world. So one has to have that respect.

But the second thing is that I have a very profound sense that because we have not been able to generate a politics adequate to the broader view that we have then we have to recognize the degree to which ordinary black folks depend on essentialist politics to preserve their lives from one day to the next. Until we can defend them in some other more expansive, more open way, we can't just crap on what they have left, on what they have been thrown back to, on the uppers of their defenses in which the only thing they have to say is, "This is who I am. This is where I stand. This is where I want to go back to. This is my defense against the world, otherwise I will drown." People play around with this as if we could just float across these spaces in our nomadic, postmodern way, sifting from here and there, borrowing from here and there. That version of openness, of the diasporic, I think is just completely irresponsible.

bell: I have tried to theorize in a way that takes one back to concrete experiences. We cannot intervene in essentialist politics if we are not willing to share the concrete strategies that we actually use in our individual lives to live better lives. This has been a real dilemma around notions of privacy and liberal individualism. What that essentialist politic keeps alive is some notion of collectivity and communalism. What the rise into a liberalist, individualist lifestyle has afforded many of us, is in fact that we don't have to share the strategies, because we are not operating in the context of communalism. We can see ourselves as operating in a very influenced, Enlightenment notion of leadership, as the leader who is apart. It has always astounded me that people don't raise critical questions about Farrakhan's living apart from the constituency that he is leading. So that whatever survival strategies he employs in order to both speak to a world of blackness, and keep alive a sense of himself as a cosmopolitan, diasporic individual, don't have to be shared because the latter side of him doesn't have to be held up.

Stuart: The two sides are neatly segregated, and both are maintained at once.

bell: Part of what I was trying to say in the final chapter of *Killing Rage* (1996) was that when I evoked a beloved community I was very interested in the work of male theorists who were saying that racism is never going to end, and we are never going to get away from it. When in fact many of us are living lives that are full of the diversity of bonds and ties. I wrote about the fact that I really believe that there are white people in my life who have divested of their racism. I don't really believe that one has to be racist in some essentialist way, but why aren't we able to build a progressive politics from this standpoint?

Stuart: I was talking earlier about the film that Jess is making. Jess is making a film in Brixton about young Brixtonians. Brixton has its image as the oldest settled black community in London, but of course it is actually much more diverse than that. It is changing very rapidly. So he is making this film about the young people in Brixton, about the diversity of people, and it has a wonderful couple, a black boy and white boy who are very close friends. The white boy is a white working class lad, typical London, who is about seventeen. He has made a fish pond with his father in the waste ground where they live. He does up cars, and he drives a little mini which is practically falling apart. This black boy with locks is an up and coming d.j. These kids met, they lived in the same house, but of course, never talked to one another, and were kind of opposed to one another. The black boy came downstairs one day and saw a group of black boys beating this boy up rather badly. He is not very articulate as to why, but he went in and stopped them. He said, "No you mustn't do that. He's my mate." Although he wasn't. Because he was black the other guys left him alone. Since then they have been bosom friends. They don't do everything together. They live quite separate lives, but when they are together it is obvious that there is a great bond between them. They go driving in the country. This kid likes the country so they go driving out to the south coast.

In the course of the film Jess asks both boys what would you feel about having a mixed race child, and both of them say, "Well, I wouldn't think of it for myself. I don't know if I could bond with the other race that way. But," they both say, "of course it's my kid so if I had it I would look after it. I'll defend it." They are sitting next to one another. They're like two lovers. They're sitting on the sand throwing pebbles into the sea. It is the most romantic moment. They have lived their lives in and out of each other's pocket. The white guy actually says, "I wouldn't be here if it weren't for him. They were going to kill me so I owe him everything. I owe him my life." This notion that they couldn't possibly have the kinds of relationships with the other races that might produce a mixed race child comes from somewhere at the top of their heads that has absolutely nothing to do with the actual lives they're all living in Brixton. Going to the same clubs. Listening to the same music. Going to each other's backyards. Standing with one another at the bottom of the staircase in the same project building. So a great deal, certainly, in England that is, of what is spoken as a kind of essentialist politics, essentialist framework denies a sociological reality which is much more complex than that. We have to speak on behalf of this because sometimes people will say, "You are middle class. You don't experience this. You don't live on the front lines." I am not suggesting that the front line is nice, that there isn't any racism there. I know exactly how much there is, but you need to give an account of it which is not just one-dimensional, that is not what all white kids, or black kids living in London, know about.

bell: That is though precisely the dilemma, and part of why essentialism is on the upswing, because the lived experience is no longer that of containment, even in the world of racial apartheid in which I grew up. Because there is a shortage of public housing, this world that was all black now has many white families moving into an all black world. So the very notion of blackness is obviously never going to be the same, because the blackness we grew up in was predicated upon non-engagement, non-involvement. You had no white neighbors if you were among the segregated black poor. It is precisely people's inability to articulate the meaning of these new experiences. What does blackness become in the context of this diversity and this variety?

Stuart: It is as if we don't have a concept of what blackness might be in the context of diversity, as if it is polarized between either blackness or diversity, but the two things can't be maintained together. Incidentally, what do you think of Henry Louis Gates' book, *Colored People*, about his own childhood?

bell: My one-line review of his book in my journal was, "Gee, this person wrote a whole book and told us absolutely nothing about his own life." I thought it was an interestingly structured book. Since I am also about to publish two autobiographies, I've been real aware of the degree to which memoirs and the autobiography has become this crucial discourse in and of itself within the discourse of race and gender. Partially through the writing of one's past someone like Skip is attempting to say, "I may be at Harvard, and I may be brokering in this academic world that is predominantly white, but here is testimony to blackness, to my roots." But it is interesting how then people cannot critique that testimony to see how much it is fashioned along a particular line, a particular line that works as an affirmation of a very static notion of blackness even as your own experience is not remaining in a static notion of blackness at all, but of engaging blackness within the context of diversity and variety.

Stuart: Do you mean by that that he doesn't talk about his own movement out of that world, or what has happened to him since?

bell: I also felt like he didn't talk about his own movement in that world. When I was sitting up in my racially segregated, Christian fundamentalist household reading my Wordsworth and Elizabeth Barrett Browning there's the imagination of a world beyond a static notion of blackness that happens prior to the movement out of that world. And I feel that in a sense it has become very unfashionable to lay claim to that imagination. In order to lay claim to authentic blackness you have to not confess to the other forces that moved you. The greatest force in my childhood, in terms of my development as a thinker and an artist, was Emily Dickinson. But for a long time I didn't refer to Emily Dickinson because there was no space for this in the project of rewriting one's black authenticity. I felt that was what was missing from Skip's narrative that willingness to write into the narrative what your own imagination of otherness is that is beyond the personal. Obviously I didn't know Emily Dickinson, but it's what she symbolizes as the writer devoted to her work. This was crucial to my development of myself as a thinker and a writer.

Stuart: There must have been things like that for him too.

bell: That was the gap that I felt in that text, and everything becomes marked by the personal encounter with the other as opposed to the imagination as a field of dreams. To me what released me from the narrow blackness and whiteness of my upbringing was the imagination of another place. To some extent, what I feel most in narrow nationalisms and fundamentalisms is their attack and their assault on the imagination. Our imagination is where our strength to resist lies.

Stuart: It is very strained, very one-dimensional. It doesn't encourage the play and the imagination. You should always have a possible other. It doesn't have to be a real place. You just need a place in the mind that one can go to. You are right in saying that that dimension is missing from the text. I guess I liked it because I thought it was unexpected of him at this moment to make that move.

bell: This takes us back to the question of why women, black women in particular, have never really emerged as the powerful prophetic leaders of movements for black liberation. While we can cite Angela Davis as a powerful icon, she's never really been perceived as a leader. That has a lot to do with the fact that, whether consciously or not, feminism has to play the role in bringing any black woman thinker, leader into greater subjectivity, into greater politicization of herself. But because this is so rejected in the sphere of blackness, to some extent, people like Skip can become the voice, the authority, the god-like father, despite their interracial relations, despite their being located in places like Harvard, because they can authenticate blackness in other ways. I saw this narrative at this historical moment being about that, about laying claim to blackness. When I think about my own story of my girlhood what people will see when reading it is how much I am influenced by these voices that are beyond notions of blackness and black identity which are the forces of Wordsworth, Gerard Manly Hopkins, the poets whose work filled my days, and whose imagination of reality was what gave me a sense of the life that I wanted to lead, and that I was moving toward. That has left something that will authenticate me in blackness. The whole construction of black woman as the betrayer of the race, as almost inherent betrayer of the race, precludes black women being able to move against the boundaries on lots of levels and still maintain the kind of positioning that allows for leadership. The most expansive thought about identity and blackness has really come from black women thinkers and again black gay theory, and yet that is the theory that is least embraced. So finally, at the end of the day, people would rather have black male leaders, more conservative black male leaders who authenticate a blackness they are familiar with than embrace the work of more visionary thinkers who expand beyond that.

***

bell: This is another conversation that we are going to have. I spoke about feeling affinity with Foucault's sense that it was hard for him to experience pleasure. I want to link that to our discussion of black intellectuality by saying that one of the profound spaces of mistrust many black people have had of the intellectual, and many people in general, is that sense of the intellectual as someone who cannot have pleasure, who is mired in an anal retentive seriousness that doesn't allow for play.

Stuart: If that is what the black intellectual looks like they are quite right to mistrust.

bell: Then I thought about W.E.B. Du Bois and C.L.R. James—

Stuart: C.L.R. James played.

bell: And this is exactly why when I think about talking to you, and the impetus I had for talking to you, I feel like part of what we are trapped in, is particularly that academia gives us one kind of discourse that is prioritized and valorized, and therefore, a certain aspect of who one is can be articulated through that discourse. Part of why I fought so hard to write both within and outside the academy is to be able to get different dimensions of one's being. It doesn't quite come through in the writing of someone like C.L.R. James.

Stuart: No, and in some of my writing it doesn't come through either, but it comes through more now than it did at an earlier stage. What this suggests is not so much that I've changed, so much as my relationship to writing has changed. Therefore, writing at one stage, writing in a serious intellectual way required excluding or expunging from the prose those things which I have always done which is to take pleasure in thinking and talking. A lot of people always find me talking easier to get hold of than me writing. I have an easier relationship with talking, lecturing and so on. It is because in speech I love the playful side of me quite a lot. Here I don't mean consciously, I mean looking back at it, listening to a tape. It's almost in the structure of the sentence. It's as if I begin the sentence and literally I don't complete the sentence grammatically. There's a kind of break, and then I find the vernacular, playful, ironic, exaggerated, exuberant way of posing the thought which is different from the measured, academic way in which I began it. But very often I suppose that is what gets edited out. Also, when I write, and I write very fast, the only way in which I can write very fast is almost to lecture silently to myself. I lecture to myself as if I am talking to an audience and write it down, and even though you have to do something with that afterward it has a certain kind of spontaneity. Now I am not talking about the relationship to writing, I'm talking about this kind of playful element, because, I must say for myself, that I find people without a sense of humor, without an ironic perspective on themselves to be just completely boring. I can't bear to be in their company.

bell: For me this is one of the aspects of institutional academics that's been very difficult, the absence of a place of humor and play. I was thinking back to our conversation of black masculinity, and how much the valorization of play seems to be essential to any project of critiquing and intervening on a notion of patriarchal authority.

Stuart: It is exactly that. The absence of any ironic view of oneself that allows the maintenance of that patriarchal politics.

bell: As I went back over the film conference I thought about how people were trying to turn you into a patriarchal icon, and how I felt completely misunderstood when I said it was possible for me to value your work, and to worship at the throne of Stuart Hall, but not in a way that I felt was resubordinating one within a patriarchal framework. I was struck by the inability of men, and largely black men, to imagine a universe where they could pay homage to the power of your thought. This takes us back to Paul's critique of the family, because they seem to be unable to do that without reinscribing you as father within the patriarchal paradigm.

Stuart: I do agree with you about that conference. It was a very bizarre experience for me, for all of us, all the Brits. The funny thing was that my daughter, Becky, was with us. We don't usually go to conferences together, but she happened to be in New York at the same time. She was absolutely amazed by it. It did make her feel profoundly different from that particular version of my intellectual life, and in part, that was due to the absence of humor, the absence of playfulness. Words were in oscillation between over affirmation and over deference, an inability to somehow come through the middle of that with its own respect which didn't set you up. It was a curious experience for me.

bell: It was an interesting location. On one hand you have a reification of blackness taking place while on the other there was a profound disrespect for the vernacular, particularly for a certain kind of wit and humor that is intrinsic to the vernacular.

Stuart: It was completely elided and excluded. It was all about the vernacular, but it didn't have any of the vernacular in it.

bell: At the heart of a lot of my fear of nationalism is precisely its desire to wipe out the spirit of play as that which disrupts, alters and transforms. In a lot of the new work I have been doing I have really tried to talk about how threatening it has been to the cause of black liberation to have black bourgeois culture become the central defining sign of freedom. I think that usually means a trashing of the vernacular, a loss of the vernacular. One of the things I remember about Skip's autobiography was the complete lack of humor. There was a stiffness in the writing itself that surprised me, because it is not a stiffness that I find in Skip as a person. In fact, one of the bridges between Skip and a person like myself is his humor.

Stuart: I thought that was a part of the world he was inscribing, and his relationship to it. He probably is in the writing, as well as in what he is talking about.

bell: The writing of blackness into a middle-class paradigm, to me, will always necessitate the writing out of the vernacular. That is why people like Langston Hughes and Zora Neale Hurston were so pitted against other groups of writers who were concerned to construct a neat, clean idea of blackness. Again, we're back to Farrakhan, and to some extent Cornel West's rhetoric is often a rhetoric of neatness and cleanliness where you don't feel there is any place for play or principles of pleasure that necessitate something other than an untarnished vision of blackness.

Stuart: There is a whole range of things that we can talk about when we talk about play, because, first of all, we are talking about being able to put oneself and one's self-image at risk. Although this is sometimes a face saving device, that is to say that if I put myself down then you won't put me down too much when actually it doesn't work like that. It opens the floodgates for everybody else. If the aim is to preserve intact a secured, corseted, or shored up patriarchal position it's not a very good weapon to come back at you.

There are other elements in play. There is the element of play which is about the dialogic, which is about the relationship with the other. It goes back to our question about conversation. Conversation is a great deal of play. There is a great deal of play in conversation. It's linked with pleasure in part because its modality is erotic, by which I don't mean just that there is a sexual dimension to it, which is true, but that is not really what I mean. I mean that a good conversation has teasing, flirting and rejection in it. It has all those moves made, never to completion, never finalized. It plays across different chord changes. A delight in conversation requires a delight in those unfinished moves which is one of the things that I like about it. I like the undermining of departmental meetings by blurring the boundaries by teasing and flirting actually in public. Flirting in public around the table with someone else changes the frame of the conversation. It can't go on in that orderly, set up way in which it was targeted, because you have just allowed another frame to run across it. You can see that, and see how they are caught half way. All of those elements are in public intercourse, social intercourse, or even private intercourse. It is the stuff of interaction—

bell: In my new book on film, *Reel to Real: Race, Sex and Class at the Movies*, I have a long chapter on *The Attendant* which is by far my favorite work by Isaac Julien. One of the things I constantly say to people is that I can't imagine any black male intellectual/academic in America being a part of such a project. What I was so struck by in seeing you in *The Attendant* is that play across the field of masculinity in a way that is not allowable in some way in the United States for black masculinity.

Stuart: The funny thing about *The Attendant* is that really I thought that it wasn't playful enough. I have appeared in more than one of Isaac's films and always they contain Jimmy Sullivan who is an angel with beautiful wings suspended from the ceiling, and I keep hoping that I will appear at least in wings. Everybody else in *The Attendant* is dressed up except me of course. I'm in my blue suit. That of course is not the point of it, and I was glad to play that role. There is something about the differences between the U.S. and here. I don't think it is that blackness here is not constituted with pleasure. The difference between the two is not as gross as that. It has more to do with the fact that all of Britain was involved with the empire, with slavery for hundreds of years, longer, in a way, than the United States ever was. There is a difference, and it is not the insane country. In the United States you are still living next door to somebody who could have been your slave master. Here, of course they were our slave masters, but the return has been so long and interrelated in a way that black people re-encounter the British as if they sort of know something about them. They are intimate enemies. They are not intimate in the same sense. They are not family. Whereas, what one knows of blacks and whites in the United States is that they were a kind of family, they were family members. There is an intimacy of everyday, ongoing life. The way that scars a relationship, and therefore, shapes the response to that relationship in how consequently it is formed. It is different from the way in which it has happened in Britain. The re-encounter between blacks and the colonial empire.

bell: So that it becomes very hard to construct a masculinity that has an element of play. In my mind flash the images of Malcolm X and the sternness of those images. There is a sense that our shining black prince is definitely not a playful prince.

Stuart: No, he is not.

bell: What will we have to do culturally to unpack that notion of playful masculinity, almost as an unreliable masculinity, because it is not the mirror of the patriarchal possibility, of authority?

Stuart: The problem is that its guardedness now is entrenched in racism itself.

bell: Absolutely. I have felt that people have not been receptive to Paul's new work that tries to show how cross sexual practice representations of the black male body have been very fixed, firm, situated as an unmoved mover. Objectification is dangerous for any future of radical black subjectivity, and not in fact, a gesture of transgression.

Stuart: Which is why of course we continually think about the film industry. Some of them do break out of that sculptural fetishization.

bell: It's interesting that we have yet to then have an image like the black male healer in Haile Gerima's *Sankofa*. That was not a film that I liked very much at all, because it embraced all of these patriarchal stereotypes of racial redemption, and yet, in the one figure of the character Mutabaruka played, there was this sense of an alternative masculinity. The pleasure that I had in that is that to the degree that Rastafarianism constructs itself as an alternative masculinity it never gets examined in the States, because there is such an overlay of associating Rastas with sexism that the element of playfulness has not received its due.

Stuart: Yes, I agree with that. It has definitely been written out. In its earlier stages it definitely had a more playful element. It was a very strong alternative image, although it had, of course, a patriarchal element inscribed in it in relation to its reference to the queen. But that was much too simple in terms of the way in which masculinity was inscribed in it. It didn't problematize masculinity in any way, but still it was not buoyed up, shored up by the armor of masculinity, or patriarchal masculinity, in a patriarchal cultural way.

bell: Exactly. In those narratives, in their profound critique of work, of certain kinds of alienated labor, there is more potential for rupture of the patriarchal masculinity than in the way the image of the Rasta now serves within a contemporary patriarchal context.

Stuart: Yes, the way in which it is not driven by the struggle for competitive advantage or the mastery, or representation of mastering the external world, but rather there is a comfortableness in just letting the world pass. These things were a very profound re-inscription, or partial reconfiguration of another black masculinity.

bell: And also they were so pleasure-centered. I suddenly have the image of Teacake in *Their Eyes Were Watching God*. Teacake, if I were figuring him in a visual imagination, would have that element of Rasta. Again, not the hard body, but in fact, the lean, vegetarian body, the contemplative body that says, "I am just content to be here by this lake for a few hours watching the water move." I have a flash of a Bob Marley concert, and the sense of pleasure, of exuding a blissful pleasure. I was suddenly contrasting that to hip hop and the sense of hardness, and the sense of a very hard, pugilistic masculinity coming through that.

Stuart: Marley brings to mind a sensuousness, a certain pleasure.

bell: I was thinking of "turn the lights down low and open wide your window curtains."

Stuart: And at the same time he is not tall and glamorous. He is quite small and light. He is very, very distinctive in his body image as the icon and the voice of that particular formation. It is very different from what has been reconstituted in rap.

bell: To have this more progressive political vision that we are talking about there has to be written into it the significance of pleasure as that which allows us to deal with difficult things. I think that this is important within feminism as well. Feminism is one of those movements that nearly choked itself to death by eliminating all possibility of humor, and of humorous and playful treatment of things that do have serious implications. Without that space of play movements lose their vigor and their capacity to be contingent. One of the things I was thinking of earlier was the notion of contingency, and how we have historically operated within political traditions that have not suggested that our paradigms of liberation have to always be contingent and changing. Our political traditions have often suggested that we could have something static which to me is always what the patriarchal family paradigm offers. It offers a static vision of freedom to be held on to, rather than a contingent notion that can say, "The family is ever-changing, never the same." Therefore, we cannot actually posit any grouping as the substantive and most powerful grouping, but that in fact we have to talk more about deeds and actions within the family, rather than the particular grouping, because the grouping, especially if we think about blacks in the diaspora, is completely changing as we look at areas of the world where you have refugee camps that are peopled by women and children. What does it mean to offer some ridiculous patriarchal paradigm as the trope of redemption in places in the world where that is just a structural impossibility?

Stuart: A kind of playfulness brings the continuum into being. It works as an acknowledgment of the contingency, of what cannot be closed, of what cannot be foreseen, of what will continue to move us on which is already present in this situation. Although it may not be in a complete, positive, affirmative voice, but the ironic thing is that there is already a negative presence already there which we can see around the corner of the formation that one is working within for the time being. That is extremely important because so many of the essentialist patriarchal forms of politics which are without this dimension of pleasure, irony and play, can't see that it recapitulates its own forms of exclusion, but they always do. All of the movements that we have been involved in have come to that moment of seeing who is not within, of moving themselves on to those people who consciously have been excluded. That outside then comes back to trouble and disturb the settled form of the subject the politics were once engaged in. That happened profoundly in relation to race in feminism. It is race that is outside of the discourse. Then it comes back, and allows some people to be sufficiently troubled by its inclusion, to rethink where they are. The static nature of essentialist politics depends very much on excluding that modality.

bell: The discourse of sexuality became such a taboo discourse within feminism precisely because in that sphere of play and pleasure it was hard to keep everything in the neat categories—oppressor/oppressed. People didn't really know how to talk about the way desire, or even a yearning for pleasure, could in fact disrupt more conventional power hierarchies so that they become something else. We are still at an impasse in having a language in which to talk about that something else, because it gives a power to play and pleasure that we want to deny.

Stuart: We don't have a politics, and this is the same point I made earlier on, but again it comes back in with a vengeance, we don't have a politics that includes that image, that includes the uncertainty of that. We find ourselves unable to think politically about what that would mean. Our images of politics are so grounded in closing the ranks, putting up the barricade, defining who the oppressor is, getting him or her, or whoever it is over on the other side, completely separate from us, getting him out of us and us out of him. The image we have of politics as this sort of mutually imposed barricade puts one in the dilemma of wanting to dismantle that, and consequently, as it were, not having any politics at all.

bell: That is exactly what has happened with all radical politics in the States right now. There is a sense that if you stand on the side of pleasure, in any way, you must stand against any kind of political allegiance which is really, really frightening. When I first heard the title of Elaine Brown's book, *A Taste of Power*, I was struck by the erotic implications of that, but also the displacement. It is not a taste for freedom mind you, but a taste for power, and the sexualization and eroticization of power. It fits with Nazism, or wherever fascism has taken root. It is that sense of the eroticization of power that precludes any notion of play, contingency or pleasure.

Stuart: It goes along with a kind of fixity, indeed there is a desire for fixity, and an eroticization of the fixed.

bell: This past year I have thought a lot about death. The death of Toni Cade Bambara really made me stop and pause, because so many black women writers have died in the last few years at what I think of as very young ages, in their late forties and early fifties. It just made me think a lot about the way we live our lives. I have been reading the letters from C.L.R. James to Constance Webb, and I have been thinking about the place of death in our culture. I feel very strongly that my life feels very changed at this historical moment by the reality of death in a way that I would not have spoken of it ten or fifteen years ago.

Stuart: I would have to agree with that, but it has to do with a number of different things which come together. Let's talk about illness for a moment. AIDS is a very particular phenomena. It is another illness. It's an illness directly related to all sorts of social situations, and it comes so unawares, and it has been so disastrously connected with pleasure and desire in the culture. So that I think it is inevitable that even if the other thing that I am going to say weren't present then one would feel that one lived constantly in the presence of death in a way in which I don't think in my twenties or thirties I did. Younger people feel that way partly because they all know people who have died. But I also think that it is a question of age, at least in my case. In the middle of my life I really did think that I was immortal. I don't mean that I felt special. I just couldn't imagine it. I couldn't conceive of it so I didn't live in the present so much. I didn't think about it so much. I didn't fear it very much either.

bell: The world of my childhood was one in which when blacks were sick they could not go to the hospital. The hospital would not receive black people. There was only one tiny, old black hospital so if you were dying they didn't want you to go there because there were only so many beds, and they were for sick people. Dying was something you did at home. Childhood was for me very much a space of death being around and very present, although it was usually of the elderly. It was still definitely a presence in daily life.

Stuart: When I was young a number of people died of that generation. I mentioned a favorite aunt of mine who I spent a lot of time with, who looked after me. She died relatively young, and since I was the youngest child in my family I felt that death very much. Then there seemed to be a period in which I didn't know many people who died. I wasn't touched by death very much until my parents started to get ill and eventually died. The death of my parents is very important to me because I didn't get along with them. I got along with them less and less. I had left home, because I didn't get along with them. I knew if I had gone back I wouldn't have been able to escape them within the small context of Jamaica, and I knew that I couldn't live in the same place as they did. A lot of my adult life has been trying to come to terms with my relationship to them, and I sort of had the illusion that when they died this problem would be resolved. But what you don't realize is that, in effect, having left home very early, that when they died nothing changed at all. All those problems I had already internalized, I had lived with an internal dialogue with these folks for such a long time that their literal, physical death didn't make much of a difference.

The more recent phenomena, the more recent experience, is about people of my own generation, and people I know well are suddenly getting to that point where people that you have known throughout your life start to die. I have seen this sort of in anticipation, first, through having Catherine's mother living with us. She is now nearly ninety and has a wide group of friends, and in that older generational way she is very careful about her old friendships. She is someone who always writes to old friends, even to people she hasn't seen in twenty years. She writes once a year or twice a year. She has that letter writing habit so there's a very wide range of people that she knows. She was married to a Baptist minister, and through the church she grew to know a great many people. She has kept contact with a great many of them, although in the fifteen to seventeen years that she has lived with us practically every month is punctuated by death so that you see this entire world fading. Like the lights going out there is an increasing darkness. She experiences that very strongly. I suddenly was aware of the fact that if you are linked into a network of a generation with interests, activities, work and friendship it's a loss that cannot be repaired in this life. She cannot make those contacts again. They are gone. It is a kind of anticipation of death almost in the dying of others.

bell: I suppose that I started this conversation with the memory of Toni Cade Bambara because for me she along with others such as Essex Hemphill and Marlon Riggs has been at the forefront of a certain kind of thinking about desire and life. I have been thinking a lot about an aesthetics of existence and about individuals that have been committed to creating a life that mirrors what they write or think about. I feel the loss of these individuals very, very deeply, and other individuals as well who I am not naming whose lives were an inspiration to me.

Stuart: That has happened to me more recently, in just the last five years. Interestingly it has coincided with my own illness. These are very often people of a younger generation who in their forties have been very seriously ill, some of them dying. If they are not dying they are now struck by an illness that is life threatening that they will now have to live with until their death. So just the awareness of that as a new dimension of the way we live with other people is a very striking reality.

bell: One of the things AIDS did was to break the social taboo around dying as a public discourse. I feel that we are much more aware of illness and death. AIDS, because of its closeness to sexuality and desire, meant that people then began to talk about illness in a more forthright way. Suddenly I am aware of the fact that so many black women get lupus. Suddenly we have a city bus in New York that says these many thousands of people die of lupus every month which is huge compared to the number of people that die of AIDS or other kinds of illnesses. Four years ago I don't know that I had heard the word lupus. Partially there is this new kind of awareness that we have, and because there is not the social taboo of discussing illness and death there's not the idea anymore that you should keep your cancer to yourself. We are now acutely aware of colleagues, friends, comrades and acquaintances who have serious illnesses that might not have been talked about a few years ago.

Stuart: That is true. I think the taboo has gone. People have spoken about the taboo of talking about death for a very long time, but they were unable to do anything about it. But in the last five or ten years it has disappeared. You have put your finger on what has made that possible. It is the combination of illness and death. It is the beginning of a whole process of death so that even if people don't die the illness reminds you that they have entered that phase which leads to death. It used to be that the discourse of death had a final and terminal moment which you couldn't speak about, but now you can speak about it because it's two, three, four or five stages on. It's particularly true with people in their forties and fifties, because that is the moment, at least in my experience, and once it happens to you, you become aware that it is happening to other people, some serious illness even if it is not life threatening.

bell: Or in the case of some feminist friends of mine whose families now talk about having what they call the hereditary cancer genes. That each family member is at risk.

Stuart: They are aware of the illnesses of their parents being something more than it once was. It is something carried by the family itself.

bell: Or talking with one of these individuals who parents with the knowledge, because she has already had cancer, and so has every single one of her family members except for one and many have died, that she may not live through her daughter's life. She parents with that recognition, and partially this can be attributed to medical technology. We didn't have that technology until recently so that at another historical moment she wouldn't have known this.

Stuart: That also disrupts the natural succession of generations. I know massive amounts of people in their forties who in the middle of apparently good health suddenly developed very serious illnesses. Some of them have died, and many have not, but they will never be the same again. They are certainly aware that they have begun the descent to death.

bell: When I was so sick a few years ago it was a turning point in my life. Until that moment I had many fantasies, not so much of immortality, but of thinking that I had a stretch of time where I could resolve a lot of things in my life. I remember also when I had a biopsy, and I was waiting to hear what the results would be. I had this forthright doctor who said, "If it's malignant basically you would have a few months to live." During those six days that I waited for the report to come back I did an evaluation of my life, and I wasn't happy with what I saw. I wasn't happy with where I felt I was. I want to talk more about the art of dying, because I had always felt, having been so familiar with dying as a child, that I really wanted to live my life in a way that I would feel at the point of dying or death that I was satisfied with the life that I had lived. It was really a shock to me in this moment when I realized that I wasn't satisfied. I felt at that moment that I had given too much of my life to work, and that there were other aspects of my life which I had not fully explored, fully given myself over to, that so much of my life between the years of twenty to forty had been focused on writing and on doing my work. I felt a real sense of panic and fear that I could possibly be near death without having lived the life essentially that I had wanted to live.

Stuart: Yes, that is what I mean by the anticipation of death. It's the first major illness that strikes in one's mid-life. It's not that one doesn't recover from that, but that it is an experience different from other illnesses that one has because it precipitates that awareness of a reckoning up of how one feels about the life one has lived. It does produce turning points. It certainly produced turning points when I was ill in the early eighties for the first time. It produced a turning point of exactly that kind. I had spent too much time working, and also I felt that I had lost control of my own life for other people. I had followed what other people wanted from me more than I had what I wanted for my own self. I was suddenly aware that I needed to stop and ask myself: "What do you want? What is going to happen if you don't finish that? Is the world going to come to an end?"

It was a very important turning point, but one of the things that it has made me think about also is that we may have to give up the notion of an art of dying which is the satisfied completeness of a life. The art of dying may have to be the coming to terms with messiness and inadequacies of the life one has actually lived. That is another way of putting it. If you think of it as an art which will complete an arch, as it were, then you build the satisfaction into it. I know lots of old people, and this is something that has struck me very deeply, that many of them are very unhappy with the lives they have lived.

bell: I just finished reading Margaret Forster's memoir, which chronicles three generations of working class women and one of the things that was so poignant and sad about her story was that she has to grapple with the fact that her mother is extraordinarily bitter as she approaches death in her eighties. Her mother is constantly stating, "My life was not worth anything. I didn't do anything." That really stunned me when I read it.

Stuart: This is quite common. There has been a certain romanticization of the whole experience of growing old as if somehow serenity always comes with old age, or the sense of a completeness of a life well lived. It does happen, and people are lucky who have a sense of fulfillment when they are facing death. But I think it would be better to prepare, to be more accepting about what can and cannot be resolved in one's life, what one isn't going to have time to do. I keep thinking about problems that I feel are unresolved, yet in a way it's too late to resolve them. You can't reconstruct the circumstances.

bell: Then that becomes a resolution in itself. When I was sick one of the things that I felt when I looked at my life was that there was a certain kind of passion, for example, that I thought I hadn't had in my life, a certain engagement with another human being that I wanted to have. Since that time I've had it, and I know the difference. I know that I did not feel I could die three years ago, and now I feel I could. It's not because that passion wasn't messy and full of problems. It wasn't the fairy tale passion where one lives happily ever after, but it was itself something that made me feel that I had completed something.

Stuart: That sense of completeness is different. That is a sense that even if the experience we are talking about, the feeling we are talking about that we want to experience, is deeply troubling or disturbing it is still better to have had them than to not. It's better to be able to reflect on them and what difference they made in your life than to never have had them because the opportunity didn't come or one didn't take them.

bell: A lot of these bitter elderly people are bitter precisely because they have lived so long and have still not been able to make the leap towards that which they yearn for. That bitterness is not only caused by having to stand in the face of death daily, because so many of them are ill, and they know that they are standing with death, that they can't stay death's hand, and at the same time they confront the fact that they have had all these years to possibly take that risk, make that courageous step, and did not.

Stuart: It is also true of people who live well beyond their generation. The ideas and ideals of the next generation retrospectively challenge the life they live. They were perfectly happy with it until along came their daughters and their sons who, inevitably, in the course of growing up had to break, construct or declare a different kind of life. That throws a retrospective light on their own lives.

bell: It's amazing, and that is part of the poignancy of Margaret Forster's book that she can chart generations of working class women who had to do so much labor. I look at my mother and think about her raising seven kids without an automatic washing machine, and what the daily-ness of her life meant just in terms of laundry, the hours of her life that were given to this chore. I wake up in a world where I have no children, things hardly get dirty, and then I have someone come in to gather those dirty things to whisk them away and to bring them back clean. It creates lots of generational conflicts that are not talked about, a certain kind of contempt my mother has for my life, because she feels that my life is in some way an indictment of the life she lived.

Stuart: The new life is an indictment of the life that she has actually lived. In a way the dissatisfaction not only comes from inside, but it also appears to come from outside. At the very moment you should be serenely contemplating the good life you've lived there are your deepest and closest relatives, friends, children, etc. declaring in the life they live what are inadequacies in yours.

bell: So do you think that the reality of death is altering the way we think about knowledge? It seems to me that at those historical moments when there was a lot of attention given to the art of dying they were also historical moments when people were dying from plagues, from illnesses for which there were no cures. Are we going to be transformed by this reality of illness and death?

Stuart: We are, and partly, of course, simply by the longevity of life itself.

bell: Which piggyback's on what we were just talking about.

Stuart: One of the things that is true about those earlier periods is that most people lived a relatively short time. People were coming to death on the whole at an earlier point in their lives. Even if they didn't actually die they were expecting to. So that the extension of life that is possible today with medical knowledge and medical technology opens up a whole new dimension. It's as if you live a generation and a bit rather than just within your generation, and that does make a difference in how we understand ourselves, how we understand what we wanted. That's another thing about death and old age which connects with this. When you see very old people who have lived the lives that they could live and are still dissatisfied with them you often ask why, but one of the things that we don't understand is how young old people feel. Even if their twenties seem like ages ago to us, it doesn't seem like very long ago to them. Just as our own childhood and youth seem so close.

bell: But what it means to be a forty-some-year-old woman right now is so fundamentally different than what it has meant historically largely because of the invention of the birth control pill. My generation, born in the fifties, suddenly, as women, found that our lives were completely transformed by the absence of the fear of unwanted pregnancy, by the knowledge that we could control whether we would have children or not. There has not been enough study and research done of what this really did to society.

Stuart: It is very profound change.

bell: It is a very profound change to female identity. There isn't this gap between generations of women now, because there is a whole way of perceiving reality that is unimaginable to women who grew up in a time when there was no fully adequate birth control. Sexuality then means something completely different. When I tell my students that at the height of the contemporary feminist movement we were still arguing about whether women could be writers, whether women could ever really write with the freedom and power of men, they are stunned. The arguments were tied to the feeling that women's relation to language and life was limited by the limitation of movement brought about by having children usually. I remember at Stanford I was studying with Diane Middlebrook, and many of our intense discussions were about the question of women and writing, and whether or not the invention of birth control would lead to this revolution of how we thought about female intellect.

Stuart: It did. It is the revolutionary change that we know relatively little about. We know about its immediate consequences, but we don't know about its consequences in terms of experience either for women, or indeed for men.

bell: Which allows us to shift from death into desire, because partially what the pill did was usher in a way that both men and women could think about sexuality differently. Here I don't want to make it seem as though I am only talking about heterosexual men and women, because if part of the stigma of gayness was that one didn't have "children," suddenly we have a world where people who are heterosexual will not have children. That will produce a leveling that has never existed historically. You are no longer able to surmise if someone is gay merely because they don't have children.

Stuart: The shift has to do with the disconnection between desire and reproduction which, of course, were never as unified as the ruling ideology wanted us to believe, but nevertheless, they were harnessed in a continuing tandem in ways that were just not the case. Consequently, desire, in general, and sexuality also, have a kind of quasi-autonomy as a public discourse and in the public sphere of conduct which they never had before this development. That is very important along with the point you make about both gay and heterosexual people not having children so that you can't mark them in that way now. In all sorts of ways in the present field of sexuality you can't tell, you can't distinguish, where in the older sexual culture these spaces were marked, fixed, unchanging over people's lives, and that is just no longer the case.

bell: What is interesting to me is how little people have noted this in the work of cultural studies in a way that really examines, in a sense, a generation gap that really has to do with complete oppositional world views. There was a horror that once shaped female lives around unwanted pregnancy, and those females have lived to see a generation of females who have a quality of sexual agency that they can't begin to imagine. This produced arenas of rage between women, misunderstandings that cultural studies and feminism have not really begun to fully explore.

Stuart: You are probably right about that, because, first of all this experience remains to some extent class bound and very generationally defined. Not only generationally defined, but also defined in terms of social arenas. In England there are still many middle-class women, who in terms of what they know and what they can afford, have no barriers to living a much more open and fulfilled life, but who choose not to for cultural and ideological reasons. It is because this question is so ideologically weighted that it seems to have been studied in most countries more in terms of the regulation of sexuality, and not so much in terms of the experience of desire. The experience of desire is much more difficult to chart, more difficult to talk about, but it is also that the shift is as much at that level as it is at the regulation of conduct.

bell: That is interesting to me, because I have been thinking a great deal about this. I have been writing an autobiographical work about that period of my life and how I came to be a writer. What I was struck by as I began to write *Remembered Rapture: The Writer at Work* was the degree to which sexuality and the exercise of desire was completely tied to how we were refashioning, in the late sixties early seventies, a notion of creativity and power. The two things tied together for us, and if we were going to have an expansive, critical and creative vision it would also be intimately linked to an expansive multidimensional sexuality. Partially, I write this in lament for the loss of that fervor and that sense of the two. People now behave as if there were never a tension between female creativity and the question of sexual adventure and agency. There is a new found interest in the Beats, and as I read their work again I am completely aware that the women who were married to Kerouac and who were involved with these men were at home taking care of the children. The whole notion of a road to the writer, adventurer is still new to the female creative psyche as one where we can now go "on the road," so to speak, without the fears of grave consequences. You might be raped on the road and have a child that you didn't want. You might be stigmatized for being a "whore." There are many different ramifications. For a while many of these things were interrogated. My concern now is that kind of rigorous interrogation of sexuality and the issue of sexual freedom seems to be absent now from both the discourse of cultural studies somewhat and feminism deeply. This is very troubling to me.

Stuart: I don't know why it's absent. It is a second generation honoree, a taking for granted what is always experienced as very different from the first time you break the barrier.

bell: It is also important to remember that feminism began to explore sexuality, but that the discussion really stopped around the discourse of S/M because the relationship of power and desire could not be reconciled along the lines of freedom. The way we had defined the meaning of freedom and the meaning of justice always in terms of equality could not be reconciled with that arena of desire where so much remains unequal in terms of who longs, who seeks, who is the beloved, who is the lover. All of those questions were not easily reconcilable so that sexuality had to be pushed back again especially within feminism, because we could not reconcile desire with the kind of neat notions of freedom that we were formulating.

Stuart: I hadn't thought of it in terms of a neat notion of freedom. I would have thought of that tension which I recognize as having to do more with this tension between desire and regulations such as the questions of S/M, equality, the use of women's bodies in advertising, the whole debate about pornography, and its relation to desire on the one hand, and to respect on the other. There are questions of freedom connected in there, but it is as if external questions of conduct took center stage. Once that takes center stage the deeper, more troubling, and inevitably ambiguous questions of desire, which just simply cannot be channeled in that regulative way, the exploration at that level, along that dimension, has stopped or has been halted. I am interested in what this means as far as men are concerned, because men have always had sexual license and a certain kind of freedom that women have not. So you might say that it's obvious that they're not so affected by the change that you are talking about, but actually I don't think that is true. The notion of freedom was always related or marked as the illicit, outside, desirable, unregulated. The heterosexual matrix stabilized one field, but there was another field. There was a split between the regulated sexual life and sexual desire. Men obviously were allowed to explore in that domain in which women were not, but they were not untied to the continuance of monogamous heterosexuality as an absolute ideal of what the sexual life was like. Their situation has been transformed also.

bell: This is exactly what people are finding hard to write and think about. The way that I was framing my statements had to do with the meaning of shifts in female sexual agency for female lives, but without linking that to male lives where so much of how male sexuality, particularly within the framework of heterosexism, was constructed. Whether you are a gay, straight or bisexual, what is still constructed even within these paradigms is a constricted and contained female sexual agency against which, or in opposition to, a male adventurism that can enact itself. What happens when you level that playing field—

Stuart:—is a nervous breakdown of masculinity which expresses itself in all kinds of ways including all kinds of violent backlash, reconfiguration, re-exaggeration, reinvigoration of certain kinds of heterosexist masculinity, on the one hand. On the other hand, a different notion of freedom, agency, subjectivity and sexuality among some men.

bell: This goes back to what we were saying the other day about creating progressive politics in a more expansive way. It is harder for us to articulate what is this different dimension of liberatory sexuality for men and women than it is for us to name how it's not working. We can name the nervous breakdown as a consequence, but we can't name the utopian moments where people really shift new ground.

Stuart: That has been more difficult. People haven't tried to name those moments partly because they are more partial. The utopian notion has been in the sense that people did imagine that within a generation sexual relations would be deeply reconstructed, and of course that is not possible. Sexuality has been partially reconstructed in some places for some people some of the time so that it's all much less utopian, much less grand. There has been a backlash because so many forces in our societies that are opposed to that trend were taken by surprise in the sixties and seventies. They were completely shocked by the amount of freedom which women seized as a consequence of this shift.

It took them awhile to recover and recuperate the ground, but they have been doing this quite effectively. Perspectives of today see the utopian ideal as more on the defensive than those perspectives of the sixties and seventies.

bell: I wonder how much of that is linked to the fact that those of us who were really trying to have fundamentally different sexual practices did not talk about those things. The relationship that I was in for fifteen years was for many of those years not monogamous, but the truth is that we really did not talk about that. When we began our commitment to a non-monogamous lifestyle I was nineteen years old, and it was at the heart of the ecstasy of sexual liberation and women's liberation. Then we were able to talk about things. We sat around apartments and dormitory rooms talking endlessly about these questions of monogamy. We questioned whether or not women could ever be free within patriarchy in the context of monogamy. I remember how much our general consensus then was that women would always lose in the context of monogamy, and that in fact one of the most liberatory possibilities for women would be opened up by the committed but non-monogamous relationship. At a certain point, by around 1980, it was no longer cool to talk about those things. Now we could continue to try to shape our lives so that they reflected those principles and beliefs, but there was no longer a public discourse.

Stuart: That is what I meant about a utopian excitement, about reconstructing the world of sexuality in this way. More people have settled for trying to make a difference in their own circle, in their own life, in their own relationships, but I agree that this is not transferred any longer into a much more public dialogue. Partly because it is not quite as easy as we supposed. It is not quite as trouble free as we imagined.

bell: It is not trouble free at all!

Stuart: Right, which connects to what you were saying about an inadequate notion of freedom. One did talk about it as if one's freedom was seized then all the problems would go away in the face of this unrolling freedom, and this is not so at all. People are more aware that to grasp the freedom as one may has its own set of consequences and costs and all sorts of contradictions. Still I think you are quite right that people don't talk about it in a way which makes it a public aspiration, public discourse of desire. This is a great shame, because in many people's lives the most intriguing and complicated ways of negotiating this space have actually been tried. Now when I say "tried" I don't mean that people have conducted these experiments with their lives, their relationships, and their marriages. I don't mean it like that, because probably those things have not even been talked about inside those relationships and marriages either. Nevertheless, there have been explorations. Take the question of jealousy. It is absolutely at the heart of any discussion about transforming patriarchal monogamy founded on the legitimization of masculine jealousy which is the emotion that follows possession and control. We are talking about people formed in an era where that culture shaped us. It is an intriguing question to ask what people have done with their enmities and jealousies, how they talked about them, how they negotiated them, did they get better at losing them. We all have rich experiences of how we ourselves have tried to deal with this. It was very often inadequate, but we learned some lessons ultimately. Yet it is nowhere available for open discussion.

bell: The danger of it not being available is we only then hear the horror story of our failure. We only hear the failure of attempts to be non-monogamous or attempts to reshape our notions of family and how you live in a household. That is actually what compelled me to think about writing more about the experience of those moments. I don't feel, looking back, that failure characterizes those moments at all, but instead incredible triumph over the ways that our parents lived.

Stuart: Yes, I agree.

bell: In the household that I grew up in sexual jealousy was so intimately linked to patriarchal domination that I came out of that household committed to the notion, even before I had feminist consciousness, of not wanting to think about desire in relation to possession. I knew that I did not want to be possessed, and I did not want to possess someone else. That was so deep in my psyche that when I encountered these ideas in feminist thinking I felt I had found a political sanctioning of—

Stuart:—something that you knew about already, knew about from a different experience.

bell: It was so important to me.

Stuart: I can't say that that's true for me. Sexual jealousy was very powerful in my family, but it was slightly tilted by the fact that my father was not a very strong patriarchal figure. My mother was the phallic woman of the scene, but that doesn't mean that there was any less of a commitment to the absent virginity of the monogamous sanction. The problem for me, before I understood its power dimensions and how those power dimensions had distorted both my father and my mother, especially my mother, and really the whole family, and affected the sexual culture of my family, before I understood any of that I had formed an alternative image, but the alternative image was of the merging of two souls. It was monogamous, but not in the same sense, because it wouldn't be patriarchal. It was Lawrencian. I had read my *Women in Love*. That was my ideal of how it could be to have a sexual relationship with someone over a period of time which would be rewarding for both people, and which would avoid the horrors that I had seen going on in my own family. That really did require the absorption of the moon (woman) into the sun (man). It was a very Lawrencian picture. Lawrence is an ambiguous figure exactly because, although he is patriarchal in one sense, he does open out a language of sexuality and desire which the first generation of family misunderstood—its power, its power to attract. That virgin experience is a very powerful experience when you go through it in your twenties, and you're looking for the soul mate. I was going to reenact a scene from *Women in Love* in my life. Only feminism broke that for me. Only feminism made me realize that this was just another version of relation. It was a good version. We were both supposed to enjoy it, to get a lot out of it. It wasn't nasty and selfish in that old patriarchal way. It wasn't power driven, but definitely the lines of subordination from masculine to feminine were deeply symbolic. They re-inscribed patriarchy. I have, I am ashamed to say, some old love letters that very poignantly express this.

bell: But then what did feminism counter this with?

Stuart: It just simply said that way of living with someone else in a sexual relationship is untenable.

bell: I felt that feminism countered, not with a different model, but with the notion that it would be inside the individual, that we would be both male and female inside ourselves. So that those two polarities were still the given polarities, but we could, as individuals, embody them within ourselves. It was the androgyny of the individual that countered.

Stuart: That, of course, was very important, the next important step, but it didn't first come to me like that. It came to me like that only as an aftermath or consequence of understanding what giving up that first model meant. What it meant was retaining the power of the emotional and sexual relationship which were not tied to a set of fixed identity positions. It's that breaking apart and the notion that we are all sexual beings, and not just in one mold, that shifted my understanding.

bell: For my generation it was the notion of androgyny, because once you had the notion of androgyny it opened up the terrain of gender-bending and crossing, because now you could have sex with a woman, but you wouldn't necessarily be a lesbian. You were just in touch with the masculine principle inside of yourself.

Stuart: That is what I mean by saying it valorizes desire, but it refused the notion that this was fixed in identity. Ever since then I have always resisted the dead enemy label. It doesn't mean anything to me, and it means less and less to more people that I know. I know so many people who have had experiences with men and women.

bell: Just recently a young, white, British woman came to talk with me, and she was telling me how she had just come out at the gay pride march, but she said, "I have been fucking these black men ever since, and I am trying to make sense of what my lesbianism really means. What does it mean that since I came out I have been having all these new experiences."

Stuart: Well, the one way not to make sense of it is to ask who am I?

bell: But this goes back to the limitations of these categories in systems of meaning, and in some way, the gesture of claiming lesbianism is a gesture of claiming sexual agency. So that once she claimed it more fully then she could expand upon it.

Stuart: She could then move it into different sites.

bell: Once you're not trying to work within something that closes you down, once you open up, it has a domino effect. That is what a lot of people did who opened up in the sphere of gay rights. They came out with this fierce claiming of an identity, but then once they claimed it they found out that the identity itself was not as closed as the claiming suggested.

Stuart: That is a very important point about so-called identity politics. Very often social movements can only advance, as it were, by constructing an apparently unified, apparently essentialized, apparently homogeneous identity on behalf of which claims have to be made, because that is the only way in which you can conduct a struggle. But within that you occupy a fictional space, because the actual space in which that identity becomes a site of agency, desire, action is much more diverse, much more serialized than that identity would suggest. I don't think one has to undermine the politics of the claim. It is better to rethink the nature of the identity or identification which is called on.

bell: I feel that everyone has wanted, in a sense, to valorize a certain kind of identity politics as essential to a standpoint from which to struggle, but we are also being prophetically called to imagine other standpoints of struggle. To imagine what it might mean to be committed to justice and to ending domination from a standpoint that does not have to start off as a fixed location seems to me to be a failure at this particular moment. One doesn't have to start off saying, "I'm gay, and this is why I support gay rights." It is a sphere of political inarticulateness. My mother called me a few months ago to say that she had read in a newspaper somewhere that I was a lesbian. She said to me, "Why do you allow people to misidentify you?" And I was trying to explain to her that it really didn't matter, because I was clear about the nature of my desire and what I wanted to do with my sexuality. I said that there was really no way that I could rush to the newspaper and say, "I am not a lesbian," that would not re-inscribe the notion that the worst thing in the world you could be is a lesbian. I said to her, "My sister is a lesbian, Mom. That is not the worst thing that you can be. It's not anything negative at all. So I cannot even begin to address this in the manner that you would like." I was struck by, again, the lack of a terminology to define where I stand, because symbolically by publicly not standing in the interest of heterosexism I immediately am then perceived as lesbian.

Stuart: This is due to the way in which the relationship between identity and a political movement is articulated in the public discourse. It is assumed that each social movement connotes an identity which is itself fixed and secure so that if you are not in this camp you must be in that camp. The political problem, the reason people don't articulate this more clearly has to do with people, in a sense, silently accepting that themselves, and therefore thinking that anyone who won't declare themselves on one side or the other is necessarily afraid or not wanting to jeopardize themselves. It is a fundamental misunderstanding about how individual identities are inscribed in the struggle to valorize a particular social position. Within the struggle for gay rights there are people who have spent their entire lives valorizing a gay identity, while others have never experienced a gay relationship, and both of those positions are potentially inscribable in this thing we call the political positional identity of those people associated with the movements for greater sexual freedom.

bell: In *Feminist Theory: From Margin to Center* one of the ideas that I tried to put forth that was not picked up was that we needed to move away from this sense of lifestyle and identity. That we needed to talk about chosen political commitments, because it was only in that sphere that we would actually, not only transcend the limitations of categories, but that we would embrace the reality of the mutability of our lives. That, in fact, we were always changing, and that many of us changed our sexual habits, patterns, etc. many times in the course of a lifetime. That the only way to move away from the demand to remain fixed and located in an immutable way would be to reject the categories. But that was the least embraced idea that feminism would not be a lifestyle or identity.

Stuart: This doesn't surprise me. You have talked before about how one of the reasons why people didn't move away from that sense of lifestyle and identity is because it took a lot of time, quite a lot of processing and talking about it, especially at the early stages to try to understand what the difference was, and how to live it. That is one reason. Another reason is that it may look in retrospect more purposeful than it was at the time. It isn't always lived as a conscious project. You move and stumble as you realize that one mode of living is not on anymore. You move to another. It causes all kinds of ruptures. It doesn't work, but nevertheless you press on and it begins to work. So that it doesn't quite feel like something about which you can give a connected narrative account.

bell: You talked in our very first conversation about how you felt you had left your generation behind in some ways, and this is an area where I feel like many of the people that I knew in the feminist movement in the late sixties, early seventies, were really trying to refashion their lives and our lives. However many of these people have now become much more committed to the nuclear, heterosexual, yuppie family model of life. I keep asking myself what happened.

Stuart: I must say that with my close friends I don't think that that's been the case, not universally so. I do know some cases where it has happened, and I do know of one or two cases where younger people have gone on to enter a long standing heterosexual, monogamous relationship that then turns out to be more conventional than I had predicted. Most of the people I know have negotiated very complicated, very changeable ways of living their desire, but they don't talk about it as if it adds up to a more general case somehow.

bell: Why do you think that is? I think it's precisely that silence that reaffirms the heterosexist paradigms of the culture. As I was saying earlier, what we hear most about is the failure of our attempts to have any alternative modes of relating. Those of us who feel like we have had successful alternative ways of relating that continue to be successful in our lives don't then get a response. For example, I have been in a relationship with someone who has a partner, and I have suggested to people that I am not necessarily interested in him giving up his partner. I would be interested in the three of us fashioning a lifestyle that would be affirming to all parties. Ninety percent, especially of the people in my generation, have said, "How ridiculous. Why would anybody go for that?" Then it does strike me as a completely different historical moment. The people that you are talking about of your generation were so much more committed to political action both in the public and private spheres than my generation of people who are between thirty and forty, who in a sense, have always been somewhat ambivalent about the sphere of political activism. This is why they have so easily surrendered the terrain.

Stuart: We were also formed in a more traditional relationship between the public and the private so although we may have been expanding with it we didn't necessarily have a language that was able to cross those boundaries easily, to speak from one to another. That is one reason. Another reason is because your experience may be that these are more immediately and obviously successful than mine are. They are troubled. They have high costs. Living against a pattern which is ingrained is very difficult. It produces unhappiness even among those people who put their hand to it. There is a lot of pain. They're talking about it to their therapist. They're talking about it among themselves. It is part of the conversation which is both a political and personal one among very close friends, but it doesn't transgress into the public domain. That is where it doesn't lead. There is a problem in this. It doesn't easily cross the domain into very public domain which can be articulated as a model. Another reason is because some of the compromises, and they are always compromises, are not necessarily generalizable as cases which can be taken to signify much larger problems.

bell: That is a useful intervention on heterosexist paradigms to say that in fact what we might have to envision are multiple narratives, multiple models, that the old notion that we can have one conceptualization, whether liberatory or not, is not enough.

Stuart: That is the most important thing of all, a pluralization, an acceptance of multiplicity, of diversity, of change from one moment to another, especially of multiple needs. We have been guilty of it ourselves a little bit by talking about desire in the singular, because fortunately desire doesn't come in one package. It's for different things, and here I don't just mean sexuality. It isn't always sexual in the same way although you can run the gamut of sexual relationships touched by it.

bell: A lot of these relationships have been turbulent, including my own, and they have definitely sent us to the therapist. The point is when it comes to overall life satisfaction I feel that we are among those folks who would stand up and feel that at least we tried to live out a certain vision in our lives.

Stuart: I agree with that.

bell: And that one has to balance the fact that, yes, there are sacrifices, there's pain. Wherever there is a lot more critical vigilance and awareness, and wherever you are processing you are likely to have much more disturbance and discomfort, because you are coming face to face with a contradiction which is why I think that the traditional heterosexist paradigm of the couple, whether we are talking about a gay couple or a straight couple, but the couple who lives a certain way, sort of smoothly and seamlessly, continues to have a much more romantic allure. In its most revolutionary sense feminism said, "We want a paradigm of mutuality, of both autonomy and togetherness." So how do you begin to have that? You can't have that without tremendous contradictions and struggle unlike if you accept the seamless harmony model which in many ways is going to be easier.

Stuart: It is not only the seamless harmony, but it is also the notion that, as I was talking before about how desire is plural, the multiplicity of desires that one has for different things at the same time could ever conceivably be fulfilled and satisfied in the same way with one relationship only. I don't know how this myth has been sustained for so long, because we know it is a myth. The heterosexual paradigm is only sustained on the basis of a fantastic myth which in reality has always been abrogated for very good reason, but it was that condensation of everything into one area, the desire for friendship, the desire for mutuality, the desire for common interests and common projects, the sharing of the experience of one's life as it changes together with somebody else with whom one has constantly lived it and talked it out, and the compromises that one has made in order to make sure that there are other areas of one's life that friendship will deal with which a sexual relationship will not. All of those things point us just beyond the notion of one single heterosexual relationship which could frame it, envelop it, enclose it in any centralizing way.

bell: Within the context of a predominantly white struggle for feminist movement that was one of the cultural terrains where so much of this was debated and worked out. Whereas black women, in general, were given a very different message which was in the struggle for black liberation we can't afford at this time the luxury of rethinking gender relations. We've got to embolden ourselves by reaffirming the status quo. That's why women like myself and Audre Lorde have been such outlaws and positioned so ambivalently by black thinkers who continue to have allegiance to patriarchy. I feel like there has been so little effort in terms of theorizing black life, either in Britain or the U.S., to look at our social relations. I have so much trouble convincing people that there must be a progressive politics of gender in order for there to ever be a successful politics of black liberation. We still haven't got that point across, rather at this historical moment we have much more conventional models of black heterosexuality standing up as a sign of our wholeness, as redemptive sign which then serves to repress and silence those of us who are actually trying to create new models of ways of being, of how to live inside. It is a political arena that still has to be confronted within the discourse of race and the politics that emerge that people are reluctant to confront. I wanted to take us to the sphere of interracial love and desire. I think of so many of the people who are at the forefront of pushing against certain boundaries, and I think again of Marlon Riggs or of someone like Bill T. Jones who precisely because he doesn't work solely with language, and that he has such a presence in the body, he has been far more open than very many other men of any race who are gay in that he openly acknowledged that he had had a long relationship with a woman with whom he had a child while he was simultaneously living in his interracial love relation of many years. It seems to me that we don't have a lot of space to talk about any of this or to talk about what it means. It is almost as if it is taboo to talk about black on black relations. On the one hand many white people act as if we have left that behind in that separatism is not the order of the day. That is another problem of language, but I do see the need for black women and men to forge new dialogues together about desire and sexuality, and the practice of living together in domestic space.

Stuart: All of this is a plea for all kinds of political confessions which is what you began talking about. I wonder about its political efficacy. This is one of the problems which one has to think about. It can sometimes come across as if one is talking about one's own life as a successful, surmounting of boundaries that nobody else has managed to come up against. There are inhibitions in these engagements, and certainly they are not just negative ones. There are also reticences that are also generational.

bell: It is important to talk about this, because the big struggle I have had has been the struggle with things I experience in my life with my parents that I am no longer interested in on a certain level, that I have long ago forgiven, and yet I feel that there is a meaning to public discourse about them. That discourse is profoundly wounding to my mother and father.

Stuart: This is what I had in mind, both about my own family and about intimate members of my family. I have long thought about things which I have not felt able or write to talk about, or to speak about publicly. It's taken a long time, and that long time is not just that I could have come to it earlier, but instead that I took a long time to talk about it. It is the fact that time lends some distance, that some of them are by now dead. I wouldn't have wanted to wound and hurt them. I acknowledge this very much in relation to my own sister who is still alive yet unlikely to read anything I write about it. This is the only time I have felt able to talk about our lives or why I have known the importance of that experience in the sense that it was happening when I was seventeen. There's nothing new to me. What is new is feeling free to speak about it. That reticence is, therefore, open to criticism. It is a reticence that as a narrative always invades somebody else's life, although you don't want to technically say, "I am going to write about us. Is that alright?" not necessarily giving them this kind of conscious veto. But it does seem right to have a sense of the things that other people would not want said about things in one's own life that affect other people. They should have some say in what we write.

bell: I found recently in a public discussion that I was trying to talk about the place of class. I was saying that I found a big difference between myself and many of my white feminist peers from privileged class backgrounds who via psychoanalysis and psychotherapy actually had something in their lives that valorized speaking outside the family about intimate matters in the family. I was saying that as a working class person, and I find this to cut across race often, there was no valorization of speaking about things inside the family outside. There was nothing. What I found in the United States was that the audience I was speaking to jumped up to violently dismiss class as having anything to do with this. I finally believe that so many American, white feminists from privileged class backgrounds were able to employ the confessional in a catalytic way for political consciousness raising precisely because many of them had had long traditions in therapy of utilizing the confessional as a point of transformation, whereas it was unprecedented in our family life for someone to go outside the family and speak publicly about matters that took place in the family. The difference too is that when I have had more middle-class or upper-class friends that have done that their parents might have been disturbed, but they can discuss it and go on. In my family I felt that I would be completely ostracized. That there was a real tangible price to pay that I was not sure that I was willing to pay, and that I fear. I fear a world where my mother and father might become so enraged that they wouldn't speak to me. I am saddened by how what public speaking I have done, as in Marlon Rigg's film, *Black Is, Black Ain't*, has actually estranged me from them, and even though in their own matrix they have "forgiven" me, it doesn't mean that the estrangement isn't still there, that a bond wasn't broken, that forgiveness doesn't come with repair.

Stuart: It's very important to see the way in which the therapeutic and psychoanalytic language has provided a way for many feminists of talking about the personal without running all the risks of talking in a more directly documentary or experiential way. It has been an acceptable code of going to the level of the personal, the emotional, the psychic while not implicating perhaps in the way in which experiential narrative does affect other people in the landscape. It is not only a question of being ostracized, of never really being forgiven for having broken those boundaries, it is also a question of the hurt it caused. In a way you draw those political lessons without, in effect, treating other people's lives as a basis of a political deduction. You can use your own in that way. I don't mind confessionals which are about me. Those don't concern me, but very few of those confessionals that matter can be limited to oneself. It is all about relationships, and so you presume on someone else. You presume on other people's lives. You are telling them things that you now understand as a result of the lives they have lived which they may not want to ever understand. Certainly in my own case that is so. I have written about my sister so you will understand the context, but it was a horrendous experience that I watched her go through. I was seventeen, and she was my older sister. I had watched this family crisis that had made her ill unfold. I knew why she was ill, because of this family in this culture in this colony made her ill. I knew that she was ill with colonialism. She was ill because of it, because of the way in which we live this larger structure inside the interior of our minds. I knew this. I could see it happening. It happened partly because I wanted to be an analyst, and I read the books which explained why she washed her hands forty times a day. I read the stuff about guilt and realized where it was being produced. Where could it possibly be being produced except in this family that had rigidly put a box around her. The only place she could go was into the bathroom where she then washed herself to be free of what? God only knows what. She never had any relationship with any other man ever in her entire life. At seventeen I understood that, and it transformed my life. It made me a completely different person. I realized a) "You've got to get out of this, because you can't deal with this," and b) "You can't ever come back here, because there is a spot just next to her, in the next bed, waiting for you."

bell: Then that is the intimate, experiential critique of repression in your life.

Stuart: The point is how do you write about this when she is trying to put these fragments of her life back together. Another point that I was going to make was that now, and over the last thirty years, we are not very close, because she refuses to see that that was what made her ill. The last thing I have been able to do is to put on paper that that is what made her ill. This would be to repudiate the only thing that holds her together which is that she had a wonderful life, and unfortunately she had a breakdown from which she never fully recovered. That made me profoundly and deeply critique and understand my family and the whole life that we were living, but she has only managed to go on living by stitching it together in a kind of myth of what it was like. We could not share, and continue not to be able to, our accounts of what happened. Up until now I couldn't write about it. Now I feel sufficiently far away from it. But I haven't felt released from the obligation not to write about it, because she wouldn't have written about it like that.

bell: This is exactly how I see the overall situation of black people in the diaspora. That our crisis is as much a mental health crisis as it is an economic crisis. There are so many ways in which, particularly the patriarchal leadership globally around matters of race and blackness, is always more willing to acknowledge an economic crisis, poverty, even a crisis of masculinity, but not a mental health crisis that would really go back to the work of say Frantz Fanon. Why haven't we taken up that work? Why aren't there hundreds and hundreds of black psychotherapists and psychoanalysts globally who are amassing a whole world of knowledge that would enable us and empower us? Precisely because in the face of that crisis we have established enabling, romantic myths about our lives, about blackness. For me that is what Afrocentrism is in its crudest form. It is an enabling, romantic, utopian myth that is enchanting to so many people precisely because it keeps them away from a recognition of the state of our woundedness, of our collected woundedness.

Stuart: That has always been the most difficult level upon which to talk about black experience, and it's also why one never stops reading Fanon. It is a level that for one reason or another he was able to profoundly see into in a way that very few people even now are able to.

bell: But it is not just that they haven't seen into it, but that they haven't wanted to investigate it. Many people have wanted to close those doors. In fact, we get, not Fanon, but the sort of crude interpretation of Greer and Cobbs in *Black Rage* that becomes a bastardized version of Fanon, but one that is not enabling at all.

Stuart: No, it is not enabling.

bell: It's not enabling, because the myth of resistance and resiliency don't allow us then to examine the woundedness.

Stuart: I agree. The accounts often have tended to foreground the capacity to resist, and one knows why the emphasis has been placed there in those earlier accounts. It's very difficult to line up all of these things, to include the notion of the pathological image of the whole black experience, on the one hand, and on the other hand, reckoning the cost. It has always been bizarre for me when I come upon such one-sidedness, because people in the diaspora have not been able to survive without costs. If nobody was disorganized there would be no people made mentally ill, no one made unhappy, no families broken up. There were psychic, social and personal costs, on and on. I do think that we have to take that dimension seriously, alongside enacting people to resistance. You are right that that particular one dimensionality is tied up with Afrocentrism.

bell: This is part of why I have challenged myself politically to try to use the autobiographical as a confessional in an enabling political way. The problem is knowing the moment when we can speak the unspeakable, when it doesn't have to be veiled in this say Toni Morrison's beautiful fiction, when we can actually say, "This is one thing that happened, and this is the impact it had on us." This young white woman was describing to me her experience of living in Brixton, and she was saying, "I am approached by four or five black men daily." She described the kinds of encounters that she has with these men, and how they move from a kind of affirmation to a state of rage against whiteness. So that there is this desire for whiteness. There is a rage against it. But there is so much laid out in that encounter, and we are not even talking about this. We behave as if the issues of interracial boundary crossing have been resolved, or that they are individuals' problems. We don't acknowledge that it remains a playing field where certain kinds of unresolved pathologies play themselves out in ways that are hard. It has been difficult. It was very difficult for me to write of my sister, who is a lesbian, that she had only had white partners. In my lightweight psychoanalyzing of her situation I felt that this was in part tied to her desire not to become our mother, not to become the matriarchal, dominating black woman. Somehow the crossing of the racial boundary was perceived as the site of rescue for her.

Stuart: I bet she didn't like to hear your analysis.

bell: No, she welcomed my analysis. She is a therapist. She did say that it was hurting to read that in a book, although I told her beforehand, while at the same time she felt that we must speak about these things. It took her a long time to be able to go to therapy herself to explore a kind of revulsion that she had toward other black females, that they were not the object of her desire, that they disturbed her. But our parents and other siblings were enraged by the writing of this. And in my case, and my case is so intriguing to me because of the different class power, one of the ways I always feel that I have to subject to critique is in the way that I have the class power to write about their lives, and they have no space to answer back to what I am saying about them and their lives.

Stuart: Exactly, that takes us back to what I was saying about the responsibility one takes on by using other people's lives as parts of narrative for one's own self-enlightenment.

bell: It is interesting how when say Michelle Wallace writes about Faith Ringgold's life, Faith Ringgold then has an equal domain of power where she can answer back about Michelle Wallace's life. Between mother and daughter there is a shared claim to language and to public discourse, but my family has no public discourse.

Stuart: Even in relation to one's contemporaries not everybody has access in that way to a public discourse, and that is a break, and I am not justifying it in one way or another, in our capacity to bring this dangerous, affluent area experience into the open. I am agreeing with you that until we do this connection between the public and the private that we talked about earlier on, when we were talking about identity, will never happen until they enter the same domain. It is a difficult area, and it is one that requires a lot of courage. I say that as I listen to you talk in public, and I have heard you talk in public in this way many times. Sometimes the audience takes it, and sometimes they don't. It is a kind of tightrope walk, a laying of oneself on the line for a political project. Not very many people are willing to do this.

bell: Which I don't even want to continue.

Stuart: But you are writing your autobiography so you are going to do more of it rather than less.

bell: It is interesting that while I used to give more public lectures where I felt free to talk, because there was no trace.

Stuart:—rather than writing.

bell: Yes, if I talked about it at a lecture that wasn't taped I felt more comfortable using experiential examples, but when it came to writing it down it was difficult.

Stuart: Then you don't have any control over it. Anybody can use it, and off it goes. It is there. It cannot be taken back or modified. I agree that is much harder. I have been through the same cycle, not exactly in the same way, but in the sense that I have come to draw on those experiences in talks, public talks, much sooner than I did in writing. I am only really now able to write about those experiences.

bell: Is it possible that more men made a commitment to feminism, and to feminist transformation, precisely because there was always that therapeutic dimension of feminist struggle. For example, when my ex and I were not resolving issues within our domestic sphere we turned to psychotherapy as a location, and we continually turned to psycho-analysis as a location of illumination. But when we discuss race or when one's turmoil is racialized there is not that immediate turning to a psychoanalytic model. In fact, I would say among many black people that there is a complete resistance to the turning toward a psychoana-lytic model.

Stuart: It is different, and feminism has made that transition easier than has the politics around questions of race. Feminism has provided certain languages in which this can happen, and that is very important. But I must say that for myself, and I think this is a generational thing, I have not found the turn to psychoanalytic language in which one uses it as a kind of code for speaking, or for exploring these issues, works well. I can't say that I find talking about it in a therapeutic mode very easy. Certainly, it's one of the ways in which my personal culture has not been sufficiently feminized. Catherine would most likely give you an account of me as never wanting to talk things through, always being suspicious of talking things through. She would see me, quite rightly, not on principle, but in practice, more hesitant about using language to talk things through. I have a sort of ancient, conservative resistance to talking things through, and also of talking them out, talking them out of resistance.

bell: At the end of talking you are still going to have to act. One of the things that we might close on is that there is always limitation in the confessional, that to confess simply without a direction towards an action is useless in the same way that I believe if someone has a practice that is illuminating they may—

Stuart:—They may never reflect on it.

bell: Right. If they can change an action by an action without having to undergo a process of critical reflection, then they are changed by the experimental moment.

Stuart: This is not to undermine the thrust of the argument thus far, nevertheless, the public discourse is weaker for the fact that those boundaries are harder to cross, and that that area of experience doesn't get talked about, and therefore doesn't become part of political discourse. Consequently, certain aspects of the whole problem never surface as something to which the movements of social justice or social liberation have to be accountable to.

bell: And the joy that those resolutions, or those workings out can bring, never then become an enabling aspect of our lives. I have been thinking about the question of depression and how there has been a failure of all the different forms of black self-determination or critical intervention so that people feel a sense of defeat, not lust about ending racism, but about solidarity among black people in the diaspora.

Stuart: I hadn't thought about it that way, but I suppose in one way I would be surprised if it weren't so. The range of defeat is substantial, and that is bound to create a sense of coming to an end of a phase of activity and interest. People feel that perhaps we should try something else. This very often coincides with certain generational changes or stages in life so that it intersects with certain key life transitions. Most of the people that we are talking about were very much politicized in and around the sixties. Think of exactly where they are now in their forties, beginning to be fifties. This is always a difficult time of transition, for men as well as for women, but particularly for men. They are at the intersection of a general dilemma of politically having tried one thing—the whole arch of the civil rights movement and all that that stood for—and seeing the disintegration and the ending of that phase of political movement, and thinking very much of their own lives as parallel to that phase—the optimism, hope and spontaneity of the early stages, the difficulties of the struggle, the solidarities constructed in those dark moments. When there is a sense of the ending or transition of a struggle that coincides with the sense of transition of one's own life that does create a depressed climate and ethos, a very personal one. And here you find a retreat, a retreat from the public, a retreat into the family, a retreat into one's coming together of private anxieties and public fears, a lowering of expectations that leads to a loss of energy, political energy, but also emotional energy.

bell: Which is why Catherine could make the joke, "To the couch, to the couch," as a witty comment about how obsessed we've become with the personal. It does seem that right now we need that therapeutic input from the couch to be united with the political.

Stuart: Yes, I am sure that that is true, and it may have been that the earlier period, being one that was although very much alive to subjective questions nevertheless did also avoid certain subjective and emotional dilemmas so that in a way they were played out in the public theater of politics and a lot of those issues never got dealt with at the personal level. Now these issues have come back to haunt and disturb us at a time when people are not optimistic about the general situation, so without really a moment of confronting those issues at the subjective level it's impossible to think of going to something new, starting something new with any kind of longer-term hope and optimism.

bell: There is so little written about black people and depression. We in the diaspora often inhabit this fiction that we are not the victims of crippling depression in our lives, that somehow we, the happy dark-ies around the world, transcended. This is a very dangerous fiction, because it leaves us without the appropriate settings to deal with that sense of defeat, despair, what Cornel West often calls nihilism. What Cornel is often describing as nihilism is depression.

Stuart: Depression and despair together.

bell: Yes.

Stuart: It is interesting that you say that, because one of the complaints of racism has always been that it has always attempted to, in a curious way, or managed to rob black people of the richness of their own subjective life. We are over determined by race, by racism and by things out there. There are so many important projects in the world to deal with.

We don't have the space for the real attention, for the complexities, intimacies, depths and serious problem of bringing the inner and outer domains together into some sort of full alignment with one another so that there has been a split which curiously we have protested when coming from the other side, but we have inhabited it.

bell: I felt this very much rereading the mission statement that Farrakhan wrote about the Million Man March, because it was as though he was saying all that we are finally is determined by how we are seen by the world, and therefore it is through spectacle that we will create a sense of recovery, a psychic recovery, though the idea that the whole world will see us as these million man strong, and somehow that will be the representation that will defeat the notion that there has been this psychic trauma that is ongoing and unreconciled.

Stuart: What it does is simply demolish and displace it once again in a triumphant way, nevertheless, it does take us away from where it really hurts in our actual lives, and where it really bides on people's experience.

bell: Which is why for me there was such a necessity of bringing a critique of gender to bear on the March, because when the spirit of triumph and spectacle ends where will these men take their rage when there are no jobs? When even if one has two Iobs that are low paying life is still very hard. There were all of these notions of the man as the head of the household who is going to get this respect and obedience, and I thought: what is going to happen when that sense of entitlement that the spectacle encouraged black men to have, again the appearance of a certain kind of self, isn't registered in the reality?

Stuart: The masculine nature of that tactic is not of course unrelated to the form which it critiques. The way that people are engaged with it, because it continues in its own terms to be a notion or a recovery of mastery, of control, spectacle, of regaining one's public standing, and it left so much untouched; which is as it were, the feminine side, the feminine side of everybody involved in that kind of experience. There was no language for it. It didn't speak to it, and it couldn't, therefore, present itself on that dimension.

bell: That is why I have been thinking a lot about why the bodies of black men have become the site of a new conservatism, because, unlike many other people, I didn't just see this spectacle as just about the reinstitutionalization of patriarchy for blackness, I saw it as an affirmation for the reinstitutionalization of patriarchy in general in the United States, that somehow feminism has dealt this powerful blow in general so that people read these moments wrongly when they see them as having implications only for race or for black people, and not for a larger cultural narrative around gender.

Stuart: It has had a specificity in the racial context. It has very much tried to or appeared to address a particular dilemma which blacks experience, but I am sure you're right in saying that the elements of the feeling which went into producing that occasion had nothing to do with registering something like man in general, but man in that culture in general, not just black men.

bell: I have been thinking a lot about the anxieties of masculinity. To what extent do they impede a certain kind of theorizing on the part of men? I am very particularly thinking about black critical thinkers, because I have been disappointed in men that I really respect, like Cornel West, around the way a certain kind of masculine anxiety blocks a vision that allows for one to think in a more complex way about family, about community, and continues to return us again and again to a heterosexist vision of the nuclear family.

Stuart: Yes, there is a lot to that. The response to that might be, and the reason why a lot of people responded to that, and to his appeal, is that namely the crisis, the objective crisis bears very directly on the bodies of black men, which is not to say that it only bears there, but it is very dramatic, and it is very dramatic partly because what one thought of as the possibilities of the early civil rights movement as very much about to what could black men in the future aspire. It is there that one finds the ending of hope, the lowering of expectations, a sense of disappointment as the rewards and the downside separate out as one discovers what benefits there are are very thinly distributed throughout the population as a whole. You can see why masculinity and the position of men has been a kind of crux which you could be tempted to think requires to be addressed in its own specificity. That is a different thing from saying that it could be addressed without thinking about the context of family, the context of relationships with women, the position of women in the black community, can't be thought without addressing those things, and that is where masculinity blocks the possibilities of a deep and profound rethinking of black community.

bell: What I think about that is that to the degree that it is masculinized in a patriarchal paradigm it precludes any movement to the couch. What I find so threatening about the kinds of narratives that are coming forth in the United States is the fact that they are very anti-feeling, anti-emotional expression.

Stuart: Yes.

bell: So that not only will they have a concrete ramification like in public policy that says, "Let's do away with welfare, black men can support their families." That is one type of fiction, but another ramification underlying this is the sense that it is a waste to try to understand the psyche or any kind of psychic trauma.

Stuart: I am sure that is true. That is how, unfortunately, we have occupied, especially men have occupied our psychic lives. We have refused those dimensions. They don't belong to us, and they don't belong to black culture, and we enforce a kind of barrier against opening those doors.

bell: It is interesting, because there is a group called Men Stopping Violence Against Women who wrote a beautiful letter to Cornel. These black men have worked in the battered women's movement for a long time. They articulated very beautifully in a short space why this kind of rhetoric was so dangerous, but they still had no voice. This struck me as a fascinating aspect of our culture.

Stuart: They spoke through feminism?

bell: Yes, they spoke through feminism, but also through years of concrete work. They were not just theorizing, but they were actually the men who had worked with men, women and children who have both been the victims of violence and the perpetrators of violence. What I found to be shocking was that so many people did not really want to hear such men speak. That is to me even more frightening in some ways than that there are a whole bunch of men engaged in the old patriarchal narrative. I would think that people would be fascinated to hear what these men are witnessing and thinking about the process to end domestic violence, but this is not the case. I heard one of these men, Thulaman, give an incredible talk at the conference of Black Men for the Eradication of Sexism which was not a largely attended conference, but it was a conference scheduled by young black men. One of the men talked about an incident in Montreal where the men left the room and the women were shot by the assassin, and this man started off by saying, "What if those men had stayed? What would have happened then in that room?" His talk was extremely moving. It raised the question of what is solidarity within feminist activism, and what does it mean that one man with a gun was able to intimidate this whole room of people such that every man left that room? And when he finished he was completely beaten into the dust by a man who basically said, "That's ridiculous. Why didn't those women die fighting?" What was fascinating about this moment is how quickly this very violent narrative was able to completely efface his point about male solidarity.

Stuart: We are dealing here with a tremendously long history of struggle which has taken different forms, although the actual or particular forms change from decade to decade, certainly the core configurations get carried on and transmitted. What gets heard and what doesn't get heard, what kind of voices are allowed to shape and carry the consciousness of a movement or a moment, what experiences are constantly marginalized have long histories of duress in them. They are not just of yesterday, and they reflect lots of things outside of the political domain. It is as if everything in the formation of people as subjects then finds this when brought to the political arena shapes or inflects the nature of the struggle in that way.

bell: In these descriptions I am suddenly struck with the image of class as what is really differentiating these groups of men. In fact, these men who work in the movement to end violence make low wages, and they work long hours. When we think about recovery and depression, the black people, and particularly the black men who actually do end up, not necessarily on the couch but certainly somewhere talking about the pain that they are feeling, are the poor and working class men who are legislated to do so. Now in the States particularly you have so many court structures, that especially in terms of domestic violence a man will have the opportunity to go through a therapeutic process or to be institutionalized so that more and more of those men are actually going through a therapeutic process.

Stuart: There you have a very big cultural difference between Britain and the U.S., because in Britain, although the therapeutic culture in general terms has grown, it is nothing near the dimensions it has reached in the U.S. It is certainly not part of the official culture of courts and legislatures so that very few people, even when it is recognized that people desperately need such intervention, are provided with a therapeutic process.

bell: As much as I could have a profound critique of AA in some ways I feel that part of the aspects of Bill W.'s envisioning of AA was that it would be free, that it would be for people across class. Particularly early on, even though people have now begun to mediate from it, there would be no separation of gender, race, class. It was believed that everyone would come and engage in a dialogue which would involve the sharing of their histories and a level of critical self-reflection in community that, in fact, particularly for poor people and working class people who don't have access to individual privatized therapy, has really been a major salvation.

Stuart: Didn't some of that have root among black people in the early days of the civil rights movement having to do also with the lowering of the level of political organization and solidarity of the struggle. I don't mean that it was organized, but a lot of it was present at the beginning of the movement. There was a lot of sharing on that level in an informal way.

bell: I think for example of the role of the church as a place of confession and reconciliation, but the black church as it has progressed has become so much more of a capitalist oriented, and therefore bourgeois exercise that the idea of coming to confession and testimony get deemphasized so that when people like my brother tries to grapple, as a black man over thirty-five, with his drug addiction, he cannot find sites in the black community, unpaid locations where he can find help. And in his case, part of why he moved to Atlanta, Georgia is that there is where you have the strongest involvement of black people in recovery movements, that is black people who run groups and who have more of an infrastructure. In Atlanta he was able to combine his own personal struggle in recovery with a larger political understanding of addiction in black life. I wanted to raise this because I do think that there are locations of hope, but part of the danger of having the discourse of race always and only mediated by a class elite, is that I'm sure that my brother has done much more critical thinking in his group where black men have challenged him about how he sees women, how he used women and how women were a part of his negotiation of his addiction and codependency than if he were getting his Ph.D. In this latter atmosphere he would not be called on to address such issues. He says himself that in thinking through his own problems of addiction and masculinity he had to begin to think about his sexism and the ways that he relates to women, but there is no academic forum that would have challenged him in this way. There is actually little access in a therapeutic session that would be free enough for him to take this approach. Thinking about this made me think about teaching, both for you and for myself, because as my graduate student has been transcribing these tapes she's been having lots of problems with her life and all the issues we've been talking about, illness and death. And she was saying, "These tapes are so incredibly helpful. You can't know what you all are doing here."

Stuart: That is why it is so important to talk at that level.

bell: And this is why I wanted to talk with you about teaching.

Stuart: Yes, but of course my teaching is different, because I teach at a distance. I don't have that kind of regular connection with my students.

bell: Except I know people who have said that their life was going in one direction, and they heard a Stuart Hall lecture that changed that direction.

Stuart: Yes, I suppose that I am regretting that. Although I have enjoyed the work that I do in adult education, I have regretted the absence of face to face teaching. I enjoy it because beyond the very public occasions teaching does give you an opportunity to cross some of these registers between one domain and another, in the domain of political involvement, in the domain of subjective experience, in the domain of private dreams, disillusionment and obsessive despair. I remember very much at an earlier stage in my life when I was involved in *The New Left Review*, and in the Café of Nuclear Disarmament, my very early involvement, even before I got very involved in questions around race and racism, and at a certain point I became completely personally exhausted, just very tired, and also depressed.

bell: Like I am now.

Stuart: I think for different reasons, because I almost lost sight of what I was doing. I would get up and go in to teach at school in the morning to make a living, and then at four o'clock I would go into the office and start to edit *The New Left Review*. I would take the last night bus home at two o'clock or three o'clock in the morning from Soho square where I would sleep a few hours and then go back into the classroom. I really had no kind of personal life at all. Suddenly, I realized that I was going to have to stop doing this or else I was going to really have a serious breakdown. Then when I had to confront the fact that there was a difference between the life cycles, movements don't stop because we are tired, we get tired rather earlier or rather later so that we want to keep on going after the moment of the movement is passed, or the movement goes on and we simply don't have the energy to do it. And it takes quite a lot of emotional support from other people to say this is the moment for you to stop what you are doing. You don't equate that with the defeat of everything else. It is a remaking of the crucial nature of the subjective moment of politics for a total sentimentalization of politics, total subjectification, submerging of politics into the personal which I don't think is right. Holding that tension and finding a group with different people with whom one can talk about those factors, or talk across them, and people who can support the transitions that don't quite fit. These are very important things, and people who get involved with political activism for a sustained period of time need to, we all need to think more about sustaining this.

bell: When you said that, though, I thought that this is exactly what I feel, but for me it isn't about teaching and *The New Left Review*. It's about teaching, and then, trying to write at the level that I have tried to write at. I have talked before about how for me my writing has been a space of activism. I have seen it as having a functional instrumental use in people's lives. To the degree that it has made political interventions within the sphere of the personal I have felt called to do more of the work. I have found that I couldn't find one piece by a black woman feminist critiquing The Million Man March, and I thought are we just simply too tired? I began to try to write a piece, and I found that I felt such despair. And I felt that I was saying the same things about race and gender and class that I was saying twenty years ago. I kept thinking that there must be a body of young thinkers ready to take on these issues, because I need to step off this for a period of time, if not for this particular critique, then for the rest of my life even. But I don't think if I did this it would be a loss to the movement for black self-determination.

Stuart: No, not necessarily, providing that there are other people who are prepared to take that up and take what has been said on. Although if we go back to the depression and the despair, these arise when one feels that either you put your pen to paper one more time or there will not be much going on out there that is connected in this way, that forms a bridge or link to the sorts of things that you have been writing and talking about. And that is a source of very profound depression.

bell: What I have been trying to find is that delicate balance that keeps me healthy. For me C.L.R. James, especially around health, is a key figure that I keep in mind of how I don't want to neglect my health. There are so many black women writers and thinkers who have gone to early graves. I keep saying to people that there has to be something unhealthy about our lives because so many of us are so disproportionately, tragically ill. It is profound to think about taking a random twenty of us to look at our health issues and discovering how many of us have them. I have been trying to ask myself what I should do to mediate this. It hasn't been easy for me to try and create a personal life. As you were speaking about your own over exertion, the image I had of myself was as someone who comes home from teaching, and then writes into the wee hours of the night interspersed with several hours on the phone with various students that I am counseling on the various directions that they want to go in their lives. As all of this is going on I begin to wonder where the space is for me to have a balanced life.

Stuart: You are absolutely right to ask this question, because this question recognizes your interdependence—political and personal. Whether you're right to think that in this context there is a regime of containment and control, I am not sure about that. We are a generation that is going to express in our bodies the impossibilities of finding that kind of balance over long periods of time. Early illness and so on have struck havoc upon our generations which we talked about before. There will always be moments of these manifestations, short periods, but it would be utopian to believe that we could ever rid our lives completely of some imbalance. The fact that we are talking about this in the context of black culture is very important, because I get the feeling that there are women who write, black women and white women, and there are some balances to be found in their lives.

bell: Exactly, I agree.

Stuart: They manage to find a familial life, an artistic life, an emotional life, a public life, and they aren't destroyed by it, but rather they mutually reinforce one another. I am not saying that they have it easy or anything like that, but I wouldn't say to them, "It is utopian." But I think for us it is.

bell: Do you think that finally it is because we are so few in number?

Stuart: Yes, and because we have had a tremendously up and down history, a history of great optimism and the prospect of change, and a history of a certain kind of coming to terms that is going to be longer, slower and less effective than we imagined and dreamt.

bell: I was also thinking of myself in relation to you, because as I was describing to a certain group of people a certain level of anxiety I always had about talking to you they expressed surprise that the "powerful" bell hooks would have anxiety about talking to Stuart Hall. Of course I went back into that psychoanalytic family narrative we talked about at other moments where you can be symbolically a father for me in a way that Fredrick Jameson is not, and that is where this weirdness of a biological essentialism comes into being, where I might relate to a white male thinker as a potential father figure symbolically, but there is never a sense that on the flesh is wrought whatever longings, traumas, what have you, that I have with my actual father that then lead me to sit with you and think, "I can't speak."

Stuart: That is exactly what I meant when I said, "At this stage of life we will carry in our bodies, and marked on our bodies, exactly the forms of oscillations of how we have lived the general condition, and that is different for us than it is for other people.

bell: One reason that I was thinking about this is because with Cornel there was a kind of sister-brother sense. We were the siblings who could get together and talk without anxiety or fear, fear of offending each other with different terminologies, different approaches. Part of the force pushing me, that makes me think that I have to work through whatever anxieties I feel so that I can talk to Stuart is in part that we have been weakened by not respecting the powers of our solidarities with one another, which is not to exclude or diminish our solidarities with other groups of people, for example the tremendous solidarities that I have had with white women activists. But I don't think we as a people have valued our spaces of solidarity. As a feminist thinker, I have been acutely aware of how much those solidarities with other women, globally and within my own community, as well as in community with white women. I can also say the solidarity I have shared with women in different parts of India, Africa and Australia shape my thinking about sisterhood. They have been part of this sustaining and supporting group of comrades. Whereas I do feel that the very competitive natures of race and gender in academe have that curious function of often leading black thinkers to feel that we are always in competition with one another, and therefore, not in the space of potential dialogue and solidarity—

Stuart: Indeed. And I believe that that is especially true in Britain. There is no critical mass in intellectual life or academia. It is very narrow. It is true that all of our work has been immeasurably deformed by the lack of solidarity, tentatively deformed. I must say that personally I have been grateful to my cross-generational alliances.

bell: It is exactly that cross-generational shift that then involves one with that mix again of whatever our family of origin issues and family dramas are, and this goes back to what I was saying about Cornel. He doesn't enter as an authority figure that I fear or that I feel I have to reshape or that I feel has the potential to shame me in the way that the sense of the father does. I am definitely one of the people who feels very strongly that we need as black subjects and thinkers to use psychoanalytic models more in our understandings of how we relate to one another.

Stuart: Yes, I quite agree with that, and I was going to add, nevertheless, in spite of the fact that those cross-generational and other kinds of allegiances do get formed into various support groups, there is also always the danger. They can turn very quickly into a struggle for space in a scarce universe.

bell: Also I was thinking about the multilayered nature of this. On the one hand I could approach you with that layer of anxiety, but on the other I definitely didn't want to have a conversation with you where we don't participate as peers and as equals. To me it has been interesting to talk about how one holds the recognition of generational differences, differences of experience and at the same time find that location where, in fact, I don't see you as the father. The more that I have talked with you the less those paradigms that have to do with family of origin past intrude.

Stuart: This is why it is important, both that one does do psychoanalytic models to understand those relationships, but that one uses it as a series of insights and metaphors that are not ultimately bound by it, because there is a way of using that in which every drama ends up reconfiguring the Oedipal drama. What is interesting in any real interaction of course is the tension between the shadow of those quasi-familial, quasi-Oedipus, quasi-sibling relationships, and other things that break across experiences and political allegiances. It is true that we come from very different generations and different experiences, but there are also a lot of very important crossing points. The whole point of the conversation is not to be bound by what separates us, but to find where those points and overlaps may be. They don't lead to exactly the same impact. They lead to homologies of insight and that is really what our interaction is about.

bell: I will always be grateful to Paul Gilroy for leaping over those constructs to say, "Actually, I see you as having much more in common with Stuart Hall than any of the male intellectual thinkers that you are often coupled with in the United States." I wanted to go back to the subject of teaching, because on the one hand while you don't have a day to day, personal interaction in this arena, the way you have taught has had an entry point where people can enter, the knowledge that what you have is available to them across such an incredibly broad spectrum. There really isn't anything like that in the United States.

Stuart: Yes, you mustn't be fooled by the fact that I said that I don't do enough teaching.

bell: No, I said, "face to face contact."

Stuart: O.K. It is not a comment about how I spend my time. It's a comment about identity. I have always wanted to be teaching which is different than saying, "I have always wanted to be in a classroom teaching." But I have always thought of myself as an educator, and I don't mean that in the sense of bringing down the word, carrying the word from which other people learn. What I mean is that I get the greatest pleasure out of those moments when from a different place and with a different experience you can open a door, or there is a way of looking at the thing, or a similarity between experience, or you can give them the handle of a concept with which they can go back to their own experiences and cut into different links. In that sense I am aware of my politics of education in a large sense.

bell: What has intrigued and fascinated me about you, because it is from such a different location than myself, is the way many of us see you as having shared the same game or the stardom that the world has been so willing to give many of us in the last few years which appears to be very much at odds with that particular political sense of one's self as an educator. In my case it has definitely not been about that, the sense of careerism that I am waiting to someday be a star intellectual. That has never been anything that I have thought about, and yet, I've had it thrust on me much more to where I have had to actively confront how that positioning of me has altered the nature of how I perceive my work to be.

Stuart: Yes, but in any case the American and British systems are very different.

bell: I am talking about that global system whereby stardom can be negotiated across the water. People love the Stuart Hall who comes to the States to give lectures and attend conferences.

Stuart: I will tell you about how I became most conscious of what you are saying, and how I chose deliberately a path that has become a habit for me. It was in the sixties, when there began to be a black politics in Britain, and involved in that in Birmingham, and to some degree in London in the late fifties, although it was much more in Birmingham in the sixties when I went into cultural studies—Birmingham was a big center of black migration—and as soon as you got involved in that politics the absolutely obvious thing was that you would be the leader. I was middle class. I was articulate. I was educated.

bell: And good-looking.

Stuart: I was comfortable in England. I could move around, and I wasn't intimidated by the institution. I knew it from the inside. It wasn't that I wasn't willing to be a participant, but I suddenly got this feeling that, it's what we call in the Caribbean "the doctor complex," it is really strong from the old Eric Williams complex that at a certain point the intellectuals speak, and what everybody says is, "Boy, I heard the doctor tell it." So this was a time for the doctor to speak. I wasn't bearing the brunt of that mythic spirit. I was glad to try and help people articulate it, but the people who were really being squeezed in Birmingham were not people like me. I thought to myself that I really needed to watch my step, that I needed to not always assume that the secretary of the organization, the secretary that was myself, could speak. I told myself, "Just hold on a bit. Somebody else will do it, and it will be much better, because they will come from a much wider range of experience to speak from than you could." There was always something else for me to do which other people couldn't because of my formations, my advantages, but not that, not that. That moment in Britain nearly reproduced the Caribbean thing where the middle-class, brown skin, well-educated boy, lawyer becomes the representative. I decided that it could not be me, that I must not participate in repeating that old pattern.

bell: I actually think that this is what is happening in the States that is not positive and not a sign of re-birth or re-awakening. I don't think it is positive that every thinker, intellectual be in an institution, because I believe institutions are, by their very nature, imposing of restrictions and limitations both on thought and action. It troubles me that all black writers, or all writers in general, want a job in an institution. Yet I feel it is so necessary to have intellectuals and critical thinkers in all types of locations to not reproduce precisely the kind of hierarchy you are talking about where all our narratives of blackness come to us mediated by a small select group of privileged black elite from certain schools. To me that is what is happening in the States that many people are seeing as extraordinarily positive move forward, whereas I am seeing it much more as a conservatizing move that is dangerous, because then we make

110

it impossible for any other class to speak the very real discourses in their lives. It was fascinating when I have been in say Atlanta where I have worked on different occasions with the black men who work in Men Stopping Violence, and I say to them, "Why don't you write a book?" Coming from where I am in the world, my sense of how you acknowledge that there are black men who have a lived reality of feminist practice is to write a book. Their sense of who they are is, like, "Let's laugh here. For one, where is the time to write a book? We get paid very little. Often the kind of jobs we do require that we are on a beeper twenty-four hours a day. And we have families, many of us, so where is the space to write this book?" It is that kind of recognition that I receive continually that reminds me to keep alive the understanding that there are multiple spaces of narrative and that books in academe are not the only discourses out there. Even in thinking of the recovery movement we can acknowledge it as a space where a certain kind of discourse is happening that may lead more black men to think about sexism and gender than a bell hooks' book. They may even lead them to my books. I want to continually validate the existence of locations like that, and not over privilege the production of "texts." I just recently read a "text" about black masculinity, and I was very disturbed because it was very descriptive in that the author was saying that this is not cultural theory, this is cultural criticism. But it was so devoid of any political analysis. It was as if somehow all this work that had come out of political struggle—cultural studies—had moved into this space of dry, over-documented narrative. Everything was documented with the right Ps and Qs, but finally, it didn't have any sense of an audience, any sense of an intentionality beyond description. This brought up for me the question of the deceit of cultural studies. When I engage work like this I feel this is not what the project was about so that what is being done is very dry, academic literary critic with culture, but with no sense of a broad base of listeners or of an intentionality rooted in the political at all.

Stuart: Of course, one mustn't take this argument so far that one obviates the possibility of having intellectuals find their space. It can't be just the abnegation of responsibility. "I mustn't speak. You speak instead." There are other things to do. It is more that there is a privileging of a certain kind of work, a certain kind of writing, a certain mode of address to people. That is one register in which work gets done, and it is presented as the only work that is worth getting done. Therefore, only those people who can engage very successfully in that are really doing anything that is worthwhile or a major contribution.

bell: I personally wonder if as black critical thinkers we're going to be able to really confront the question of class in relation to black experience, in the diaspora in general, but certainly for my own location, in the U.S. I question whether we will actually address this growing sense that the true fact of America is that very few people from poor and working class backgrounds are able to get PhDs, and that we will see even fewer of those individuals in the future. I find it interesting that so many people are going back to Du Bois invoking the talented tenth but not the essay where he is critical and takes apart his own utopian belief of the talented tenth, that they would serve the people, that they would desire to be educators, that they would want to share economic and educational resources, and begins to question that whole structure. As much as there is a grass roots black nationalism that is served up to the poor, what is being served up to privileged class black people is this new vision of the intellectual as the doctor who will speak.

Stuart: I very much agree with that. This is a very serious issue. I have been trying to think about the way in which patterns are emerging distinct to this particular period in the nineties in black British culture which very much has on it the mark of an inner class structure that has not been a custom here before now. I see it much more sharply in the states, where the whole problem is different because it is played out on a much bigger stage. Here everything is so much later that the common position of black writers has submerged the class issue for a while. They haven't obliterated it, but they have submerged it. Inevitably, it's like watching a template come through the development process, a photographic solution. You see the class factors begin to play and appear on the page, between different minority groups, black between Afro-Caribbean groups . . . class fractions . . . The minorities who are able to have a perspective of writing in the social strata now have a very different attitude to this whole project of black culture, as opposed to the majority . . .

bell: What disturbs me in the States is the way it is disguising itself. There was a time when we could not talk about a black academic, or any academic for that matter, making a million dollars a year, but the irony is that as there is this kind of class cleavage that there is a certain way that blackness is being evoked as a solid. The idea that Cornel West, Louis Farrakhan, Jesse Jackson, and all of these black male leaders must somehow come together, despite all their differences, around this category of dealing with race and racism. As an aside, when I wrote my piece about the Million Man March, I talked about the fact that in Farrakhan's mission statement he says very little about racism and white supremacy, and actually everything he is talking about is gender. This I found very fascinating, because the disguise is the crisis of racism is so bad that we have to ignore all of our other differences and come together in some kind of racial solidarity. But I feel that this is bullshit, because it is class solidarity that is drawing these people together and their desire to protect the very class interest that on one level they are critiquing.

Stuart: There has always been a problem feeling the specificity that race gives to everything. We have never really managed successfully to find the political language to talk about race and class adequately without reducing one to the other. It really requires a complex analysis.

bell: That is really what William Julius Wilson begins to try and do in *The Declining Significance of Race*, but because people so often objected to that very idea without reading the book that they couldn't actually see that what he was saying was not that race was not important, but that it was going to be increasingly mediated—one's status, one's position—by class. He was absolutely right.

Stuart: Yes, many people completely misunderstood the thesis of that book. He has a new book out about the urban poor which will go back to that same assertion.

bell: Partially because his was a conservative analysis and a conservative positioning of that knowledge it then wasn't going to galvanize or radicalize, and this was a way that people could render it more suspect. I have been increasingly trying to talk about class in my work, and a critique that I am trying to raise that I haven't thought through enough is that among a black privileged class, what I have seen among a black privileged class, is a complete unwillingness to talk about a life of dignity and integrity that may be lived in poverty. Part of what happens is that the privileged class of black people, as much as they may critique the Horatio Alger image, the notion of individual rise to fame, glory and economic power, also then participate in this same fiction by acting as though the only good life is a life that is lived in material plenty. This becomes a negation of the reality that most of us live. If we realize that most of us are never going to reach material abundance, then does this mean that most of us are not going to have meaningful lives? I am distressed then because this becomes a way of obfuscating class by talking about racial uplift in terms of material acquisition. There is a denial of the class narrative of values, about what the good life is. If in fact the good life is only the life that is lived in the nice house with the nice car and so on then how are we going to talk about bringing it into black on black violence in poor communities. Because we have already said that they can't have a good life without material plenty.

Stuart: Yes, it is a big dilemma, because you do run the danger of sounding as if you are trying to reconcile people to the classic exclusions that actually exist which is not what one wants to talk about. On the other hand, it has to do with a very contemporary and reduced materialistic notion of class. I don't think anyone would have said that about black communities in the past. They wouldn't have dreamt of saying it.

bell: I wouldn't be here talking to you if we had not been told continually that the fact that we were working class and that our parents had come from poor backgrounds in no way inhibited the expansion of our horizons.

Stuart: The question has something to do with class, the particular way in which class now is so much tied to a certain kind of monetary sect, a certain kind of rapid new rising style system, etc. It is in that context that a certain kind of "good life" of that sort which can't be lived without an enormous amount of material underpinning. If that is your image of the good life then you are bound to think that that is the only measure of what you can do with it. In relation to an older point of reference, people understood that the lack of material opportunities was a very serious disabling force, but they didn't believe that that meant in any way that people couldn't live a decent way, an ethical way. Questions of the good life, of ethical choices, of holding aspirations for one's children, of giving children the inner moral sense of right and wrong, some way of making sense of the world in terms of its value, all these things could be transmitted wherever in the social scheme you were.

bell: This is exactly why I see the rise of the right and the Christian right as having such an impact on black Americans because it is only within the sphere of fundamentalist Christianity that you get any negation of the idea that material excess is the only way to a happy, value-laden meaningful life. I am continually struck by the testimony of those black people who were a part of the Jim Jones cult who said that it was the only place they'd ever been where they weren't judged by race, where class was not an issue. Everyone was being asked to divest of material privilege. For me those are very interesting movements, because I feel that my own understanding, historical understanding, of racial solidarity, is really being called into question by this shift of more and more black people to the right. The fact is that in the United States many black people support the death penalty, many black people are antiabortion so that a lot of the progressive agendas that in the sixties I would have just assumed black people would have supported . . . For example, in the sixties if you did a survey about women and work, black men were much more likely than white men to say that they felt women should work, but if you did those surveys now that we have a much more conservative notion of family and manhood permeating all classes you don't get that kind of response.

Stuart: I'm not sure that that would be true in England, partly, because we are not so strongly afflicted by the Christian right, although it is growing in its importance, and it is going to grow more. For instance, we are going to have abortion as an issue in our general election for the first time, certainly since abortion legislation was passed in the sixties, so it is coming. And I don't mean to say, of course, that there isn't some relationship between the Christian practices in certain churches and a deeply conservative social outlook.

bell: If we think about the music that is transcending the globe—rap and certain forms of black popular music—there is a very conservative underlying message. If we think about Prince, our radical, androgynous Prince, is now saying he has found God yet again, and the big issue of his life is having a baby, so that there is this whole sense on all cultural spheres, and especially on the sphere of black popular culture, that many of us have in the past seen as always on the edge potential.

This is being mediated now by the fact that there is wealth now in that sphere for a conservative black popular culture voice. This would not have been the case in the past when part of how blackness registered its presence in the sphere of popular music was through transgression.

Stuart: You are right about that. The bizarre thing is that these things don't translate from one sphere to the other so that you can still get a kind of aggressive/transgressive chronicle in certain rap. A deeply conservative aspect of that culture, the general climate encourages them to be more perverse or up front. I am very much aware of groups of young black men, very much in tune with their own blackness. They are not apologetic about their blackness. They are very much tuned into that orientation of black culture, to popular culture, to black music. You have absolutely conventional notions of success, very straight, heterosexual notions of sexuality and relationship which prescribes to "the family code." Although they are not planning it out there on the streets, nevertheless, what they subscribe to publicly, what they ascend to, what they valorize has a very, very conservative take—on sexuality, especially.

bell: I wonder if anyone has ever done any work on whether or not this is what happens when you mainstream. In a sense we can see, just as we can see a speaker like Cornel West who when spoken of before was accompanied by words like "socialism," "the left," and there was a sense of political transgression. Now if you amassed the latest ten newspaper articles that referred to Dr. West and something he is saying there would not be that kind of reference.

Stuart: Cornel is certainly conservative in our sense.

bell: No, but I just mean in terms of language. It is much more the language of liberalism. I am just trying to suggest that part of what mainstreaming does is to require a certain kind of conservatizing move.

Stuart: Remember that we are in a political era in which liberalism has virtually become the only political language which has validity. The only language in which it's worth conducting, all the debates I've conducted somehow, take place within the framework of a liberal position. This is not only true of black politics, but of politics in general. It is the only horizon left. And although of course vis a vis a conservative, particularly gender liberalism is a good thing. On the side of how bold are their alternatives which it sketches out, how rich are the utopians which it signals it is an extremely limited and very predictable place.

bell: One of my students called to report that she is in a graduate class that is dealing with film, and they are reading a lot of stuff, but not bell hooks. The critique given when this is brought up is that I am just too out there. Also, when Michelle Wallace did her critique in the paper mocking that jargonistic phrase I use, "white imperialist capitalist patriarch." But that also was referring to the reality that we might have to sustain a critique of capitalism. Black academics are as eager to suppress as any other group.

Stuart: This is one of the shifts that has taken place. What we assumed, which was, just to go back to the class issue, if you take the intersection of race and class far enough you would encounter at some crucial point the necessity to ask what is the anti-capitalist dimension to what you are saying. The same is true of poverty. The same is true of inequality. It doesn't necessarily mean everybody is a Marxist, or everybody is a socialist, or anything like that, but that there was clearly a point when one had to engage with the whole distributive system.

bell: Part of my coming to you and to Britain, and to black British thinkers and others is to be able to engage that—

Stuart:—That difficult situation, but also descending into the liberal miasma of the most radical people. The most radical people argue their case, even if in cases when you know them, you know that their cases come from somewhere else, but actually that comes in terms of making up the division somewhere where there is liberalism. That is what it is like living in a post-1989 world.

bell: That is why some kind of diasporic solidarity becomes all the more necessary for our survival.

Stuart: Yes, but I really do have to warn you—

bell: Go ahead.

Stuart: That the language of radicalism that is alive and well over here is not due to the case that people have skillfully nurtured and garnered it to make it available to a diasporic space.

bell: Do you think that I am being too hard when I would argue, like for example in your own case, that had you had this kind of mainstream stardom, that part of why you haven't had to mute your voice, is that you haven't been trying to have a constituency, or a fan club.

Stuart: Yes, that is true, but I didn't say that it has to do so within the mainstream. In many ways in comparison with a lot of black political figures in Britain I am seen as heavily compromised with the mainstream. It is not that. I think that I am aware of the fact that the negotiation with the mainstream is a danger zone. I am very aware that I don't get it right all the time. But I am always conscious that this is a negotiation. This is a very careful strategic, tactical operation . . . One chooses to go to the mainstream if one takes the opportunity. Sometimes one wins, and sometimes one loses. It is not an open space. If you occupy it too long without thinking about what you're doing you'll find yourself gliding into respectable language which smooths down the rough edges of the critique, and so on. The mainstream shouldn't keep us out of it, but it shouldn't keep us in it without some strong critical sense that you need all your wits about you.

bell: I wouldn't say that I haven't engaged the mainstream with my work, but I have tried to do that without surrendering the language of radicalism, of new thinking and the appeal to do more than theorize. We have to live in engaged ways in our lives. Ultimately, the test does not lie there in our theories, but to the degree to which we are able to groom these theories into concrete strategies for our lives and not simply the eloquence of how well we theorize.

Stuart: A formal performance.

bell: I wanted to close by talking about where is the place of love in all this.

Stuart: I knew that we would come back to that.

bell: Paulo Freire has really consistently talked about the relationship between dialogue and love. I have been thinking about how I move closer to you through this dialogue, and to some extent if we go back, and you will have to share with Catherine how much we have used her metaphor, back to the notion of "to the couch," what is the couch on some level, but this location of critical, investigative, reflective dialogue. I want to raise that, because there are so many conversation books being done now that for me there is a kind of sadness because they have been done so many times now as a commodity gesture that I want to place the nature of this conversation in the level of struggles for solidarity. I want to establish that recognition that it is important for black men and women to dialogue within a terrain that includes a poetics and erotics of relationship, but also in a terrain that is not about that, not about that I want to catch Stuart Hall or be with him in a sexual or erotic way, but whether one can in fact see the value of men and women, and in particular, black men and women relating in other ways and enhancing who we are.

Stuart: You are right to say that love is at the center of that, because love is many things. It is also a conversation, the right kind of conversation. It is also a pleasure in the fullest giving birth to conversation. It has something to do with the nature of the inventiveness that one brings to conversation of that kind that somehow can get lost, and its boundaries dissolve as something new arises which is neither one nor the other, but a space in between.

bell: That is exactly how I felt in this conversation with you. It has been very different than my conversation with Cornel. To some extent I very much organized those conversations with a series of questions, whereas you and I have just plopped down, gotten our drinks, and said, "oh, the topics that we can draw on are depression, love, death."

Stuart: Yes, people have asked me what are you two talking about, and I say, "oh, you know, life, love, death, sex."

bell: I keep thinking about jazz as a metaphor for this conversation, and the notion of improvisation, in the sense that one of us says something and the other person responds, but it doesn't have any kind of planned format.

Stuart: Yes, like jazz always does, it has a kind of improvisational approach.

bell: It has riffs.

Stuart: It has an inner logic which allows improvisation to take place. It is like jazz, also, in the sense that I can never explain it to people who don't really like it. They argue that you can do whatever you like in jazz, and you certainly can. You can do both what is within the form and yet different from it. It is constantly speaking its own absence of structure, while, nevertheless, not being just free floating and playing whatever comes into your mind. Most of jazz, most of the jazz that I like, I don't actually like absolutely free form jazz for exactly that reason. Though it is wonderful in terms of creativity, what it is missing is exactly the tension. This is about something, this conversation is about something so that it is not just can I speak nicely about this? It is about trying to get closer to truth or insight. Can I take this further than where we were when the conversation first started? There is something at stake. There is something invested in it which gives it a type of structure, a type of push or direction, which nevertheless doesn't prevent its going in this direction rather than that . . .

bell: Part of the intervention that the conversation makes is to counter the hegemony of the critical essay. The loss of a popular pedagogical model was through the academicization that led to the linking of tenure to the writing of a certain kind of academic text that therefore has no relation to the notion that we actually serve the masses, that we don't just serve the students who can pay to come to our classes. A weariness that I have felt is when people ask me to write twenty pages for their journals, but what if the ideas don't reach for twenty pages? What if they can be said in a few paragraphs? This model we are using allows for that, and therefore allows for a more popular access.

Stuart: I hope so.

bell: Certainly, *Breaking Bread* proved that to me, because so many people have said to me, "I can come home from work and open this, read a page and feel that some ideas come across."

Stuart: And you didn't have to sit down and read twenty pages and the footnotes. That is really true. It is a more openly woven form which does allow people to come in and out, to enter the conversation at different places. A lot of the time we have had third and fourth participants in our conversations, various people and traditions that we have talked about have entered the conversation. We have had to acknowledge their presence.

bell: That is why I think of it as an alchemical process where it burns away a lot of the excess, and what you get, if we use another musical metaphor, is a high note, but it hasn't come in a spontaneous way, but it has been sought after in a multiplicity of locations that reaches its peak in our space of dialogue. It is like being able to play a basketball game with someone who is as engaged with the game on the same level that you are so that you cut through a lot of things, the movements that you might have to make if you were playing someone on a different level.

Stuart: Yes, you cut out a lot of excess baggage, which is fortunate. Again, academia, despite its precision of thought, its privileging of rational modes of argument, it still has an enormous amount of crap saddling around it. When you look at the work that people are doing in the academy the amount that is really being said is about one fifth of the actual number of words you have to read. So I hope that we are doing something different here.

I will go back to saying that all of these are ways of, not only talking about the way that love depends on reciprocity, not of a simple kind, but the way in which love and reciprocity are just impossible to talk about. Also, and this is very cliché, in the way love is about the loss to the other and the voice from the position of the other. In all of those ways I have always felt that dialogic is the model. It is the model of love. That doesn't mean it's the only model there is. It is positive in some ways for those who command a dialogic mastery.

bell: There is a certain generosity of spirit that many people perceive you as bringing to those public spaces where we are invited to engage much in competitive monologic lectures. The fact is that even when we are on these panels of four and five people very little dialoguing takes place. Much more often a competing for primacy of voice occurs, but you always, in those spaces, try to sustain a space of generosity, learning and critique. What I share with you that I feel has been part of what has brought us together is what I see as the ecstasy of ideas. One of the things that I have felt very much is that my engagement is with ideas, and is not with the space of being a public intellectual.

Stuart: Right. It is with the ideas.

bell: And that is where the rapture is for me. You know when I think of you and I as a basketball game I think of you and I going flying down the court with a particular idea. It is interesting to me that without you or me contriving it to be so that this gap between the initial series of conversations and this latter one, even that gap has been part of a movement because so much has happened in the space of that gap.

Many people have spoken to me sneeringly and said, "Well, I hope that you and Stuart Hall are going to do more than just lick each other," which was fascinating to me because this image of Stuart Hall and myself licking each other is quite the spectacle to conjure up. What does this mean that people create these images around a cross gender dialogue? I would presume that when people heard that Cornel West and Skip Gates were doing a dialogue together that it didn't first come to their minds, "Are they going to go at each other? Is there going to be conflict?" But why is it that when we cross the gender divide people immediately hope that there is going to be this conflict?

I also want people to understand that in the ecstatic play of ideas there are underlying conflicts, and I think that this gap has been a place where we have thought about some of those conflicts. Then when we come together the conflict stage is not necessarily the stage that dominates, but it doesn't necessarily mean that it hasn't been there.

Stuart: No, of course not. Otherwise the dialogue from the same position is a complete mode of narcissism. But it is always a glitch in the machine, which isn't necessarily sharply opposed, competitive staging of wars and maneuvers around this position and that, etc., it's a gap that overlaps, repetition with a difference which takes advantage of that tension and movement of the prior conversation, and this makes it exciting. The one thing that is for sure is that it will not end where it started, and it won't end where it had predictably appeared it might have.

bell: It is very moving to me that we began this series of conversations with a certain evocation of home, and both spaces of conversational dialogue and interaction within those locations. And it is interesting that to some extent I feel to be able to talk with you is a return. One of the things that I often think about Fanon, that I feel created a flaw in much of his analysis was his inability to return home. I always have felt that if he could have brought his critical mind set home again and then back on the journey we would have had a much deeper analysis.

Stuart: Yes. I suppose so. I mean I don't want to disturb the sense of completeness, but I think less about home than you do. I believe that home is where love is.

bell: Yes, I think love is where one is home, because there is the site of possibility where a lot can happen. When there is the conflict in the space of love there is also the will to process often from a naked space of difference and complete unfamiliarity. I don't know how far people go with one another, and maybe this is because I have been thinking a lot lately about ruptures, endings and loss that it seems to me that part of what is in danger is our will to pursue with one another a certain movement.

Stuart: I agree with that, but then I wonder why you talk about a return to home.

bell: I use "home" very synonymously with recognition.

Stuart: I have less problems with that.

bell: When I see Isaac Julien's film on Fanon, I think for example of incompletion, in the sense of someone caught, who's never really found the location of recognition, who was always in this space of longing.

Stuart: That lost state of recognition is consonant with giving up home.

bell: Yes, but feminism has been a site where there has been much more critical discourse of home, of keeping home but revising our notions of it. So for me it is not the home of Kentucky, it is rather the making of home, in the sense of recognition.

Stuart: In that manifestation I agree with you, especially once you mention making home. I don't mean that in talking about home that you have meant simply or literally going back to your Kentucky origins, but I do feel that you have a sense of continuity with that space.

bell: Well, I don't. I feel I have a sense of romance, and romance is not continuous in that sense. Romance has its dark and strange spaces. But I do hold a notion of the union of different locations that become the making of home. It's not the single location, but it is a romance of what comes into being within the mixture.

Stuart: I had to live without romance, without those coming together. The refusal of it is deeply intrinsic to where I've been able to live. It's almost a refusal.

bell: But it might be that at this stage of your life there is going to be a return.

Stuart: No, because of entropy I couldn't physically return, because it would not be a return. The only time that I have ever felt that I could return, build a house and move back to Jamaica, is now, because it is so different from what I think of as where I began. It would be like living in a nice place, a different place. It is the distance from that location that would enable me to go back.

bell: Where you leave me then is pondering whether or not men are now more willing to engage a different discourse of home, one that is not about the need to run away or move away.

Stuart: I don't think what I have done would be entirely about running away, though it happens that in my case it begins with that. It begins with that cut, but after that I don't continue to feel that I would run away from that. Although I do feel that I would run away from that the moment it seemed I was going to stay for too long. That is about the only thing that would get me on a boat.

bell: Maybe for me, because home has always been a location of transgression, I don't think of home as a place that I ran from. I will leave this dialogue wondering if it isn't a gendered difference in our understanding and conceptualizing of home.

Stuart: I don't know that I would want to stretch it to that. I am aware that you don't have this kind of feeling. What I am saying is not a recommendation, it is not a general assumption. It just happened in my own case that I think I know that about myself. It is as if, and of course this is not true, it is as if I began again as a subject when I didn't want to be at home anymore.

bell: And maybe I say home was a transgression because I never was "at home, at home."

Stuart: Here our stories do converge. I suppose it was because I could not be like that there. I had to refuse it, because it was not a space of transgression or freedom. I couldn't conceive of any possibility for myself except for the ones that had already been preordained, because of that I had to move it. Now, of course you are perfectly right for a man to linger longer, because where does he move in order to try to find the right kind of home which one didn't find in the one that was given to you? But then nevertheless, I think I know certain enough if it ever offered itself, if it said, "Here it is. Come home to it," I think I would have just enough sadness that I would have to say no.

bell: Certainly, it is that search for true romance and a certain kind of vision of home that has been the setting for me to pursue our conversations.